JANINE SAINE

SICILY

A WAY OF LIFE IN 50 RECIPES

RECIPE PHOTOGRAPHS: PUCCI SCAFIDI

AMBIANCE PHOTOGRAPHY: JANINE SAINE

TRANSLATION: JANE DAVEY

Green Frog Publishing

Table of contents

Antipasti | Appetizers 20

Fried Olives 20 ❦ Fried Zucchini in Sweet and Sour Sauce 22
Roasted Peppers 23 ❦ Chickpea Pancakes 24
Crepes Stuffed with Spinach and Ricotta 26 ❦ Fried Cheese 27
Stuffed Rice Balls 29 ❦ Caponata 30
Mountain Fennel Fritters 33 ❦ Lemon Shrimp 34

Pane & pizza | Bread & Pizza 40

Maria's Bread 40 ❦ A Truly Unusual Sandwich: *Guastelle* 40
Pizza Dough 43 ❦ Artichoke Pizza 44

Zuppe & insalate | Soups & Salads 50

Bean and Barley Soup 50 ❦ Green Vegetable Soup 51
Orange and Fennel Salad 52 ❦ Seafood Salad 53

Pasta & risotto | Pasta & Rice 58

Basic Tomato Sauce Recipe 58
The Secret of Pasta *al dente* 58 ❦ Dried Tomatoes 58
Pasta with Tomatoes, Eggplant, Peppers and Capers 59
Pasta with Meat Sauce 60 ❦ Norma's Pasta 63
Pasta with Sardines 64 ❦ Pasta with Ricotta and Pistachios 66
Pasta with Zucchini 67 ❦ Magda's Pasta 68
Palermitan Pasta with Lentils 69 ❦ Pasta with Shrimp 70
Sicilian Rice 71

To my mother, for her culinary inspiration and love of life.

At the conclusion of numerous stays in Sicily, I send my heartfelt greetings to all the people of this island who welcomed me, one and all with warmth and generosity.

To Angelo Rindone, born in Sicily and now living in Montreal, a million thanks for having been the first to rekindle my passion for Sicily.

My warmest thanks to Peppé Giuffré and Vincenzo Conticelli for their culinary creations; Anna Liza Romano, Assistant at the Ristorante Giardino d'Eden in Trapani; Adele and Antonio d'Ali Statti, from the Marsala salt works; Pietro D'Ali from Erice; Hassan Carlo of the Charleston in Mondello; Mamone Cosimo, a Mondello fisherman; Salvato Nuzio, of the Calogero restaurant in Mondello; Alfredo Barbera, President of the Club Costa Ponente, in Capo Gallo; Rossanna Lo Piano, of the Framon Hotels; the Rindone family in Leonforte; Franco Pignataro from the City Hall in Caltagirone; the Marquis Fabrizio and the Marchioness Carolina Serafini Degli Abbati Trinci, for my stay at their inspiring villa in the heart of Palermo; Bertram and Larine Amerasinghe, for their unending devotion; Antonio Perciabosco, for his hospitality; Professor Giuseppe and Maria Anna Cascio, as well as Giovanni and Veruska Cascio, for such a warm welcome in San Elia; Karine, Amalathas and Pierre Saine from the Spaghettata restaurant in Montreal and Maria Zingarelli for their culinary testing; Franco Calafatti and Flavio Zamarella for their precious collaboration and Catherine Saguès for her final touches.

In addition, I send my friendship to Gaetano Basile, a Palermo anthropologist and ethnologist; to Natalia Ravida, a Memfi oil producer, and Francesco Spadafora, a Virzi winegrower who, during our encounters, dared to share the latest Sicilian gossip with me.

To my daughters, Virginie, Noémie and Florence, thank you for your patience and affection.

Grazie mille a tutti… e viva Sicilia!

*M*y first foray into Sicily was in 1998, when I landed in Palermo to write a report on food and wine.

From the moment I stepped off the plane, this island, the largest in the Mediterranean, made a startling impression on me. Was it the incandescent light that shimmered on the sea, my amazement at the sight of rustic landscapes from which emanated such sublime scents, or was it the genuine warmth of the Sicilian people? I cannot remember exactly, but from these first revelatory moments, I fell in love with this island.

Over the course of my numerous stays in this heavenly country, I learnt that the daily rituals of the islanders stem from the influence of several ancestral civilizations with very rich traditions, all of which resulted in the highly colorful way of life we witness here now.

I invite you to discover the gastronomical delights available throughout magnificent Sicily. On the menu, simple, healthy recipes for vegetables, beans, fruit, fish, meats and sweets. These concoctions are the creations of Peppé Giuffré, chef of the Ristorante Giardiano Eden in Trapani, and Vincenzo Conticello, owner of the Focacceria San Francesco in Palermo. Their dishes will satisfy everyone, from Mediterranean cooking experts to vegetarians.

Buon appetito!

Janine Saine

In the springtime, the Sicilian landscape glows with tender abundance.

The Culinary Influences of
SICILY

*I*n spite of its integration with the rest of Italy in 1860, Sicily continues to assert itself as a distinct nation. Embraced by the Ionian, Tyrrhenian and Mediterranean Seas, this island, whose uniquely strategic position made it the target of several conquerors, abounds with historic, agricultural, viticultural and artistic riches. Over the course of the centuries, a unique way of life was born and the cuisine resulting from the many cultural influences on Sicily would produce a diversified and truly flavorful diet. Thanks to generous sunlight, fertile soil (varying from volcanic to clay-limestone), and especially to an enduring culinary tradition, Sicily is a Mecca for both lovers of Mediterranean cuisine (so prized in the West) and those who crave simple, healthy cooking.

Stunning Sicily! In no way does it resemble any of its neighboring islands, being the only one that can boast of having three great living culinary traditions. Whether it be street cooking, the people's cooking or dishes handed down from the aristocracy, every recipe is so uniquely Sicilian that it can be created in many different versions. To get a real sense of Sicily's contemporary culinary richness it is necessary to conduct a brief historical overview of some past influences.

A Brief History

No trace of what the first inhabitants (the Siculi and the Sicans) of Sicily ate 10,000 years BC has ever been found. But from studying the rupestrian paintings discovered in the Mount Pellegrino grotto near Palermo, we can surmise that they ate whatever nature had to offer, meaning roots, herbs, honey and small game.

In the VIIth century BC when the Greeks conquered Sicily, a virgin island with a mild climate, lush natural surroundings and an abundance of forests, they were convinced they had found Paradise. Reputed to be fine gourmets, the Greeks' main contribution to the island came in the form of grapevines loaded with fruit that was crushed with bare feet on large rocks. A lot of wine was consumed during this era, even though it was fairly acidic. To neutralize the product a bit, wine makers would dilute it with seawater, which made it more stable and kept better in jars. In Homer's *Odyssey*, we are told the story of how Ulysses and his companions crushed grapes underfoot in order to inebriate the Cyclops. This enabled the sailors to perforate the creature's eye and make their escape.

Thanks to the Greeks, another Sicilian fixture was brought into play: the olive tree. It was considered sacred and became an inexhaustible supply of life force and nourishment. The wood from the tree was used to create kitchen implements and the oil extracted from the fruit was used for cooking food, healing wounds and intestinal problems, cleaning the body and making candles.

The Greeks made stews, grilled and fried foods, and bread. But they also knew the art of salting food so that they could preserve meat, fish and olives. Their diet also included rice, bananas and lemons, discoveries

world and the source of a mellow wine that is highly coveted to this day.

The arrival of Tunisian fishermen in the IXth century marks a turning point in the culinary evolution of the islanders. Fish couscous, for example, is a traditional dish as popular today in the Trapani region as it was 1,200 years ago.

Agrodolce, a sauce made with vinegar and honey originating in Islamic Persia, is a source of Sicilian pride. This country's religious doctrines dictated that human beings must always find a perfect balance between the sun and the moon, darkness and light, sweet and sour. The fact that to this day Sicily remains the realm of sweets and desserts is due to the Arabic influence, which created, among other treats, *cannoli* and *cassata* (the two most famous offerings).

In addition to bringing onions, pistachios, peaches, cherries, grenadines, the alembic, paper, alcohol and architecture whose vestiges can still be admired today in Palermo, these conquerors made their definitive mark by installing canal systems which in turn allowed agriculture to take off by leaps and bounds.

Along with the Tunisian Muslims came the Jews with their kosher foods that would quietly influence the preparation of 60% of Sicilian dishes. In order to respect their religious laws (such as not consuming seafood), the Jews developed the art of combining tomatoes in numerous pasta, fish and meat recipes, although the latter ingredient was rare and expensive at that time. Thanks to the Jews, Sicilians would learn how to sauté vegetables with cereals in olive oil and garlic. They would also learn to use all parts of a vegetable, such as the zucchini whose flowers, fruit and even leaves (when they are tender) can all be eaten.

The Normans, who came to Sicily during the XIIth century, introduced Sicilians to the chimney. This allowed the people to deal with wintertime humidity in their homes and gave them an essential tool for roasting meat. Their background, this time the genetic one,

mistakenly attributed to the Arabs. One ancient Greek dish that is well liked in Sicily to this day is *maccù*, a bean dish flavored with olive oil.

Around 200 BC, the Greeks were overtaken by the Romans who, according to history, didn't bring anything new to the island. But they did learn the art of salting fish and meat and they exported wheat, the sundial and public bathhouses to the Peninsula.

The Byzantines invaded Sicily during the VIIth century and didn't bring much to the culture as a whole except for the Malvasia vineyards they set up on the Eolian Islands. Malvasia is one of the oldest vines in the

Statue on the famous piazza Pretoria in Palermo.

would also be affected. It's always something of a surprise when you run into pretty little blond, blue or green-eyed children in the streets of Palermo or in the Sicilian countryside. This is how the Normans left their indelible mark over the course of centuries.

During the next 300 years, the Spanish would reign over Sicily. At this point in time, wine asserts a much stronger dietary presence, especially around the Etna where strong red wines were produced, and also in the Palermo region where lighter brands of white wine were made. During this period, Sicilians started exporting products such as wheat, barley, wine, oil, cheese and sugar, Venice being their main market. This was also a time when pubs abounded and nuns in convents devoted their time to pastry-making, thus becoming pillars of the Sicilian sweet-making tradition.

Since 1860 — an exceptional year during which Garibaldi landed at Marsala to unite Sicily with the Italian nation — to this day, the three types of Sicilian cuisine have remained the expression of a truly unique way of life… as if Sicilian families had invented the art of mealtime happiness.

The three types of Sicilian cuisine

In 2050 BC, in the *thermapolions* located in the agorae of ancient Greek cities in Sicily, the first type of Sicilian cuisine, *buffitieri* (derived from buffet) was born. Vendors sold ready-to-eat food right out in the streets. This type of cuisine still retains a certain kind of prestige, as it is Sicily's most ancient tradition. Sicily can actually boast of being the first country to have created a *take-out* or *fast food* industry, offering people pre-cooked food such as fried fish and boiled or grilled vegetables to be savored on the spot or taken home. Born out of necessity and invented by illiterate people with tremendous creative drive, this type of street cuisine has survived from generation to generation, to this day.

The second type of cuisine, called **popular**, was maintained by the Sicilian women. It was "poor man's" cooking that was qualified in Palermo as a kind of "spiritual reinvention" of aristocratic cuisine.

What was happening, in fact, was that servants working for the nobility would tell their wives about the dishes they had witnessed being prepared, although these men may not have tasted a single one. In both cities and the countryside, people would attempt to duplicate these aristocratic dishes, often with lower quality ingredients. *Caponata* is the crowning achievement of this type of popular cuisine.

The third type of cuisine is termed baroque, aristocratic or *monzù* (sir) — the latter being a Sicilian expression referring to the French chefs who came over during the XVIIIth century to prepare sophisticated meals in the nobility's palaces. This cuisine had a certain inherent masculine element, since it was indeed concocted by men. Sea perch, capons, sole, quail and rabbit were an important part of the bourgeois diet, while poorer folk satiated their hunger with vegetables, beans, pasta and sometimes fish that was more or less fresh, depending on your means.

The Beauty of
SICILY

Located only a few nautical miles off the coast of the Italian peninsula, Sicily has maintained a truly luminous way of life throughout the ages. The country's splendidly diverse heritage, baroque cities, stunning landscapes, coupled with the warmth of its inhabitants, makes Sicily a multifaceted but very accessible nation.

But don't mistake a Sicilian for an Italian. Should this happen, despite their discreet sense of humor, Sicilians will be rather upset as they feel very strongly about their roots. They will be even less impressed if you bring up the Mafia. It's not that the subject is taboo, but you will certainly be reminded that the phenomenon exists in other parts of the world as well. To really understand the Sicilian soul you must understand, first of all, that it is an impressive amalgamation of several different cultures. The Greeks, the Arabs, the Spanish, the Normans and even the Bourbons (of Naples) were all to profoundly influence a way of life that is as evident today in the architecture as it is in the cooking.

PALERMO'S CHARM

Your first stop during any trip to Sicily should be Palermo. Getting up at dawn is a must if you really want to feel the frenetic pulse of the Sicilian capital.

What a joy it is to stop at a *caffè* to drink an *espresso* (one of the best in Italy, incidentally) before you set out to explore the winding streets with their ancient facades. Go to the Capo market where tender artichokes, Barbary figs, plump red tomatoes, aromatic herbs, swordfish and *dolci* are piled up on the stalls in a delicious abundance.

For Palermitans, the heart of the city is the Quatro Canti district, which boasts an array of baroque houses embellished by statues and fountains. There you can feast your eyes on churches, palaces, the water basins on the piazza Pretoria, the Martorana church's Byzantine cupola, the Arab-Norman style cathedral and Palatine chapel, the Norman palaces, as well as the Arab masterpieces in Sicily's regional art gallery. All of these historic hallmarks are well worth your time.

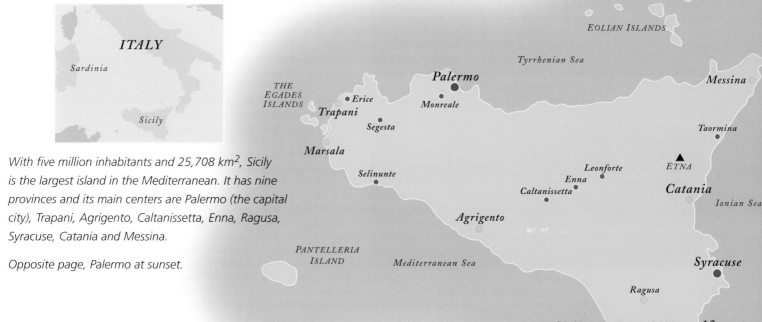

With five million inhabitants and 25,708 km², Sicily is the largest island in the Mediterranean. It has nine provinces and its main centers are Palermo (the capital city), Trapani, Agrigento, Caltanissetta, Enna, Ragusa, Syracuse, Catania and Messina.

Opposite page, Palermo at sunset.

From top to bottom: the neo-classical style Politeama Theatre; the Arab-Norman influenced cathedral; one side of Mount Etna.

ANCIENT TREASURES

Once you leave the Arab-Norman influenced Palermo and go west, you're in for 500 kilometers of extremely pleasant roadways before you hit Syracuse, a city that is definitely of a more Grecian style. Inland, the countryside is mysterious and undulating. Places such as the austere city of Enna, surrounded by wheat fields, lead the visitor into a contemplative space. Meanwhile on the coast, seaside attractions and small fishing ports such as Porticello or Cefalù on the north coast, will bathe you in an ambience awash with the blue intensity of the sky.

On the east coast, you'll encounter the medieval city of Taormina with its Tropezian flavor. At the heart of this ancient city you can enter an impressive Greek theatre offering a magnificent panoramic view, spanning from the Etna to the Ionian Sea. If you want to climb Mount Etna, a well-known, still active volcano, you can go by either the south slope or by Taormina on the north slope.

From left to right: a street in Old Palermo; the Greek theatre in Taormina; the Doric style temple in Segesta.

Once you've reached a certain level, you will feel you are walking on a black moon and, as you go further up to 1,500 meters, you'll find an oasis of orange and lemon groves and even some pinot noir (a well kept secret).

Further south, Syracuse welcomes you with more eye opening sites such as the sculpted facades in the via Vittoria Veneto and the superb baroque cathedral built next to the ruins of a Doric temple. On this grand archaeological site in the Neapolis district, you can admire one of Italy's largest amphitheatres, a Greek theatre carved into the rock, and the *latomis*, ancient quarries providing stones to build the temples and the palaces.

When the road forks off to the left, the traveler will pass by Agrigento, Selinunte and Segesta before encountering some truly amazing sites, including the intact remains of Greek temples. The remarkably well-preserved Temple of Concord in Agrigento, erected during the Vth century BC, remains a model of elegance and harmony.

The island's western tip opens the way to Marsala, which means God's port in Arabic. With its pedestrian streets and animated market place, the city center is extremely pleasant during the day. But when the sun goes down, this divine city becomes totally tranquil.

Towards the northwest, laid out over a majestic rocky outcrop, is the medieval city of Erice, whose ramparts date back to the Norman Conquest. When evening falls, a stroll through the city's interconnecting alleyways plunges us into a strangely monastic silence.

A stop at Monreale, south of Palermo, is a must for any visitor if only to pause and admire the cathedral and cloister displaying the remarkable artistry of the three main cultural influences: Arab, Byzantine and Norman.

The village of Erice: top, the Castello Pepoli e Venere (Norman style, XIIth century), and below, the Chiesa Matriace (a XVth century church).

Island Getaway

North of Messina and bathed by the Tyrrhenian Sea, the wild beauty of the Eolian Islands is a sight to feast the eye. Hovercrafts departing from Milazzo take you to Vulcano, Lipari, Salina, Stromboli and Panarea. You might be tempted to stop at Salina to see the house where the film *Il Postino* (The Postman) was shot. There, on the terraced hillsides, are cultivated the best capers in Sicily and Malvasia (a sweet dessert wine). The seafood you can taste in the small makeshift cafés is so perfect, you just know it's the freshest possible. If you want to tour the island, rent a Vespa or use the local bus service. It's a paradise for nature lovers!

Religion or Superstition?

In the heart of Sicily, on the Etna coast, lies Leonforte, a village with a distinctly provincial flavor. Before Holy Week begins, a highly theatrical religious event called *Ecce Homo* takes place. Pacing themselves to the rhythm of melodramatic music played by the local marching band, hooded repenters, young and old, carry Christ to an encounter with the Virgin. Marvelous Sicily, where religious beliefs are still so ingrained, they actually seem to serve as a protection against modern life's insane pace.

A Sicilian Gem

A few kilometers off the coast, in eastern central Sicily, is the very pretty baroque city of Caltagirone that was rattled by earthquakes during the XVth and XVIIth centuries. There are ceramics to be seen everywhere in the city: on the walls, in the Museum of Porcelain and Ceramics and in restaurants and boutiques. The city's pride and joy is la *scala*, a vertiginous staircase consisting of 142 steps, covered with ceramics in 1954. On July 24, when the Festival of Lights takes place, this staircase is lit up with 5,000 olive oil candles.

Beautiful, impressive Ragusa! Built on a rocky outcrop and rich in baroque architecture, this city also offers many enticements for food lovers to discover. Here and there, the tantalizing aromas of pistachios, almonds, oranges, lemons, grenadines, carob, wine, cheese and olive oil exhale memorable aromas.

Olive fritte
FRIED OLIVES

SERVES 4 TO 6

8 oz (250 g) large green olives

½ cup (125 ml) breadcrumbs

1 cup (250 ml) extra virgin olive oil

2 salted anchovies

2 eggs

Pit the olives and set aside. In a frying pan, brown half of the breadcrumbs in 4 tablespoons (60 ml) of olive oil for a few minutes. Combine the anchovies, fried breadcrumbs and 4 tablespoons (60 ml) of olive oil in a food processor until you get a homogenous paste. Stuff the olives with this mixture.

Dip the stuffed olives in the beaten eggs and roll them in the remaining breadcrumbs. Fry the olives for a few minutes in the remaining olive oil. The olive oil's temperature must not exceed 350 °F (180 °C).

Avoid commercial breadcrumbs, as they often taste of cardboard. Homemade breadcrumbs are very easy to make. Simply grate finely some dried bread (such as a baguette) or put it through a food processor.

As much as possible, buy anchovies sold in glass containers rather than the canned ones.

Delicious at cocktail hour with a glass of white wine.

Zucchine fritte in agrodolce FRIED ZUCCHINI IN SWEET AND SOUR SAUCE

An inexpensive simple-to-make, but oh so tasty dish! For a little extra aroma, add some basil leaves to the zucchini.

SERVES 4

4 medium-sized zucchinis

5 tablespoons (75 ml) sugar

½ cup (125 ml) white wine vinegar

½ cup (125 ml) cold water

1 cup (250 ml) extra virgin olive oil

Cut the zucchini into medium sized slices and set aside. In a frying pan, melt the sugar over low heat. Add the vinegar and water and stir until boiling. Remove the mixture from the burner.

Fry the zucchini slices in the olive oil until golden brown. After absorbing excess oil with paper towels, place the vegetables on a serving platter and cover them with the sauce mixture.

Peperoni alla griglia
ROASTED PEPPERS

SERVES 4 TO 6

8 peppers (preferably red or yellow)

Extra virgin olive oil

2 cloves garlic, crushed (optional)

Wash the peppers and place them on a well-oiled tray. Place under the grill or, even better, roast them over the barbecue. Grill the peppers, taking care to turn them over as soon as exposed skin starts to blacken. Remove from the oven, pull off the blackened skin, cut the peppers in two and scoop out the seeds. Then slice the peppers in strips, cover with olive oil and the two cloves of garlic.

This is the most classic way to prepare peppers. I've been told that in the past, it was customary for grape-pickers to get up at dawn and roast peppers on the embers before starting the grape harvest. If you consider that the pepper is in fact a fruit (because it contains seeds), even though used in cooking as a vegetable, then these morning pickers already knew the art of concocting flavorful breakfasts as vitamin-filled as they were colorful!

Panelle
CHICKPEA PANCAKES

SERVES 4 TO 6

6 cups (1 ½ liters) water

17 oz (500 g) chickpea flour

2 tablespoons (30 ml) sea salt

½ cup (125 ml) Italian parsley, chopped

1 cup (250 ml) extra virgin olive oil

Panelle *is a diminutive of the word bread (because of its thin texture). Sold in markets and other public places, this dish originated during the Greek* buffitieri *era when food was sold ready-to-eat in the streets. Today in Palermo, you can still buy it on the streets. A truly tasty appetizer (or snack)!*

Bring the water to a boil, add the chickpea flour and salt. Cook for 20 minutes while stirring to obtain a firm, smooth dough. If the dough is too thick, add some water. Add the chopped parsley. Spread the dough on a marble surface or on an oiled dripping-pan and let cool.

Cut the dough into small triangles or squares 3 in. x 3 in. (8 cm x 8 cm) and fry them in olive oil until they are golden brown.

Chickpea flour is usually available in natural food stores.

The use of Italian parsley is optional but it does add a nice, fresh touch.

The photograph to the left shows raw panelle while the one to the right shows fried panelle.

Crespelle di ricotta e spinaci CREPES STUFFED WITH SPINACH AND RICOTTA

Typical of the Syracuse region, this dish is traditionally made at Christmas.

SERVES 4 TO 6

10 oz (285 g) spinach (rinsed and with stalks removed)

1 lb (450 g) ricotta

Sea salt and pepper to taste

9 oz (250 g) white flour

2 eggs

1 ¾ cup (435 ml) milk

Steam the spinach for 1 minute. Drain well and cut into strips.

Mix the spinach into the *ricotta* and add a pinch of salt and pepper.

Place the flour, eggs and milk in a bowl and beat until smooth. Heat up a lightly greased frying pan and ladle in enough batter to obtain a circular shape. Once the crepe is golden-brown underneath, spread on some of the *ricotta* and spinach mixture. Fold the crepe into a half-moon. Remove from the frying pan and place it on an oiled cooking tray. Repeat the process until you run out of batter. You should obtain about 6 crepes.

Place the crepes in a preheated oven (325 °F/160 °C) for 15 minutes.

Formaggio fritto ou cacio all'argentiere
FRIED CHEESE

SERVES 6

6 slices pecorino or caciocavallo cheese

½ cup (50 g) flour

1 cup (250 ml) extra virgin olive oil

Red wine vinegar

Oregano

As popular as it is classic, this antipasto was created in Palermo. Legend has it that a banker created this recipe after experiencing a reversal of fortune which left him without the means to make aristocratic dishes. The fried cheese was the answer to both this man's hunger and his misfortune.

Dip the cheese in flour and fry it in the heated oil till golden brown. Place the fried cheese on paper towels. Just before serving, sprinkle with red wine vinegar and (if you wish) oregano.

At the island's core, in the province of Enna, Turidou Patti, Turidou and Angelo Gagliano make saffron and black pepper pecorino.

Arancini
STUFFED RICE BALLS

SERVES 4 TO 6 (APPROXIMATELY 10 RICE BALLS)

One of the most popular and classic dishes in Sicily, it is also sold individually in market places and other public spots. In the Syracuse and Catania regions, they make rice "ovals", while on the rest of the island, the balls are nicely rounded and orange-sized, hence the name arancini *(small Italian oranges).*

1 small onion, finely chopped

1 tablespoon (15 ml) olive oil

4 ½ oz (125 g) ground beef

¼ teaspoon (1 ml) salt

2 oz (50 g) fresh or frozen green peas

3 tablespoons (45 ml) tomato paste

12 oz (350 g) arborio or carneroli rice (avoid using instant rice)

1 tablespoon (15 ml) salt

¼ teaspoon (1 ml) saffron

¼ cup (60 ml) breadcrumbs

3.5 oz (100 g) diced mozzarella or other melting cheese

3 eggs, beaten

1 cup (250 ml) olive oil

Sweat the onion in olive oil. Add the meat and salt and cook for 10 minutes. Add the green peas and tomato paste and cook for about 10 more minutes until you obtain a thick sauce.

Cook the rice (with the tablespoon of salt) according to directions and drain. Once the rice is at room temperature, add the saffron (diluted in a little hot water beforehand). Mix well until the rice becomes a light yellow color.

On a table, place (separately) a bowl of cold water, a plate of breadcrumbs, the diced cheese, the meat mixture and the rice. Take some rice in your hand and shape it into a half-ball the size of a medium orange (rinse your hands in cold water first so the rice doesn't stick). Form a hollow in the center of the half-ball and insert a tablespoon of the meat and pea blend and a few cubes of mozzarella (or other melting cheese). Close the ball with more rice and round it off with humid hands.

Once you've made all your rice balls, dip them one by one in the egg mixture and then in the breadcrumbs. Fry the rice balls in heated olive oil and drain well.

There are several variations on this recipe. The ground beef can be replaced by ham or you can omit the meat altogether and stuff the rice balls with cheese cubes only.

CAPONATA

SERVES 4 TO 6

4 Italian eggplants (preferably small and firm)

1 tablespoon (15 ml) salt

1 ½ cups (375 ml) extra virgin olive oil

3 peppers (preferably red), diced

2 celery stalks, diced

2 tablespoons (30 ml) capers (rinsed if preserved in salt)

1 large red onion, cut in julienne strips

12 green olives, pitted

½ cup (125 ml) white wine vinegar

1 cup (250 ml) tomato sauce

2 tablespoons (30 ml) sugar

Cut the eggplants into large cubes, salt them, and leave to sweat for 30 minutes.

In the meantime, heat the olive oil in a large, thick-bottomed pot and fry the following ingredients separately (in that order) until golden brown and slightly crunchy. Start with the peppers. Once these are browned, place them on paper towels. Repeat with the celery, capers, onion and olives. Brown the eggplants last, as they absorb a lot of olive oil.

In a clean pot, place all the fried ingredients together and add the vinegar, tomato sauce and sugar.

Cook for 10 minutes.

Serve cold.

Caponata *comes from the Latin word* caponae, *which means tavern. During the XIIIth century, it was forbidden to bring wine or vinegar aboard Sicilian ships headed for the open seas to forestall drunkenness among the crew. In came* caponae, *which were cottages of a kind, located near the ports, where one could get a sauce made with honey and vinegar. Since food was limited to the* galetta, *a hard and inedible bread, the sailors would dip their rations into this sweet and sour sauce. Hence the term* caponata. *The popular version of this recipe is prepared with olive oil, vinegar and vegetables.*

Another legend gives the monzù *credit for this recipe. The* monzù *were French chefs working for Palermo's nobility. The former were supposed to have concocted a mixture made of vinegar, capers and white olives, intended mainly to preserve capons, hence the origin of the word* caponae.

The rich prepared this dish with fish, pine nuts, celery, raisins, pear slices, artichokes and vegetables. Today, there are more than 37 caponata recipes and these may contain ingredients as varied as fish, crab and hard-boiled eggs. The recipe we have provided was inspired by a popular version. The best accompaniment to this dish is a slice of bread.

The western version of this recipe is reminiscent of ratatouille and of the sweet and sour flavor of chutney.

Frittelle al finocchietto di montagna
MOUNTAIN FENNEL FRITTERS

Mountain fennel or finochietto di montagna (not to be confused with fennel root) grows wild in Sicily on clayey soil, ideally at an altitude of 1,500 to 1,800 ft (500 to 600 m). If it grows at a higher level, it is bitter, and at a lower level, it becomes hard. Picking time is usually in March. This herb is difficult to find and can be replaced by dill, although the latter herb's flavor is not as intense as wild fennel's.

Makes an excellent appetizer because it is light, tasty and economical. It's also fun and easy to make.

SERVES 4 (APPROXIMATELY 8 TO 10 FRITTERS)

1 tablespoon (15 ml) fresh yeast* (or 1 packet dried yeast)

1 ⅓ cup (300 ml) hot water

2 teaspoons (10 ml) sugar

7 oz (200 g) all-purpose flour

5 tablespoons (75 ml) wild fennel or fresh dill

1 cup (250 ml) extra virgin olive oil

* Fresh yeast can be bought in bakeries or gourmet food stores. It is preferable to use fresh yeast over dry.

Put the yeast, water and sugar in a large bowl and mix well. Let stand for 5 minutes. Add the flour and stir well until you obtain a smooth, semi-firm dough. If necessary, add some more water or flour.

Steam (in a vegetable steamer) the fennel or dill leaves for one minute. Shred them and add to the dough.

Heat the olive oil in a frying pan and drop 1 large tablespoon of dough into the oil so that the fritter is formed. Repeat the process until you run out of dough. Fry the fritters on both sides until golden brown and place them on paper towels. Keep the fritters warm until serving time by placing them in the oven at 200 °F (100 °C).

Gamberi al limone
LEMON SHRIMP

If your shrimp are very fresh, I'd recommend that you serve them raw. With frozen shrimp, I'd advise you to use the cooked version of this recipe.

SERVES 4

Raw version:

14 oz (400 g) medium-sized gray shrimp

¾ cup (180 ml) lemon juice

¾ cup (180 ml) olive oil

2 French shallots (gray shallots), thinly sliced

1 teaspoon (5 ml) capers

1 teaspoon (5 ml) sea salt

4 tablespoons (60 ml) red wine vinegar

1 ½ tablespoons (20 ml) thyme, fresh or dried

2 tablespoons (30 ml) Italian parsley, chopped

Lemon zest

½ Romaine or curly lettuce, cut in julienne strips

Sea salt and pepper to taste

Shell the shrimp and marinate for 5 hours in a mixture of all the ingredients except for the lettuce (the shrimp turn pink when in contact with the marinade). Drain (but reserve the marinade) and arrange shrimp on the julienne sliced lettuce. Pour 1 tablespoon of marinade over each shrimp.

Dip some bread in the marinade while you savor your shrimp… a simply divine sensation for the taste buds!

Cooked version:

4 cups (1 liter) water

14 oz (400 g) shrimp (preferably medium-sized and gray)

2 lemons (yellow or green)

3 fl oz (90 ml) extra virgin olive oil

Sea salt and pepper to taste

Chopped parsley to taste

Boil approximately 4 cups (1 liter) salted water and add one sliced lemon. Once the water has boiled, remove it from the burner and add the shrimp. In a matter of minutes, they will expand and turn pink all while remaining slightly crunchy.

Drain the shrimp and let cool. Shell them and squeeze a lemon over them. Season with sea salt and pepper. Serve with a trickle of olive oil and chopped parsley.

During the IXth century, when Tunisian Arabs occupied Sicily, they encountered Sephardic Jews. The latter led quiet lives and their diet was governed by strict religious laws. The most rigid of these laws concerned sea products; these could be eaten only if they had scales, fins and bones. This immediately prohibited the consumption of crustaceans and shellfish. Even the Sicilians ate little of these because they found them difficult to shell and not very nourishing. During the XVIIIth century, however, a few gourmets started eating gamberi (shrimp), crayfish and mussels. These eating habits are still very much ingrained in Sicilian culture. So much so that shrimp are not part of the popular menu and are considered an aristocratic dish to be eaten only on occasion... most likely in a trattoria, especially when you are invited by a host who is generous enough to offer you some.

A THICK-CRUST TOMATO AND SALAMI BASED PIZZA GARNISHED ACCORDING TO WHIM, *SFINCIONE* IS EATEN ON THE STREETS. THROUGHOUT THE SEASONS, SMILING *SFINCIONE* VENDORS SHOUT THEIR WARES IN THE PALERMO MARKETS OF VUCCIRIA AND CAPO.

Bread
HEAVENLY FOOD

*I*n Sicily, bread is considered sacred food since it is often made in conjunction with religious celebrations. There are more than 200 existing varieties of bread, including the following yeast-based creations: the bread baked on February 3, feast of San Bagio (who protects the population against sore throats); the round loaf produced in the Palermo region on March 19, feast of Saint Joseph; the Easter egg bread that is given different names depending on the region; the product made for the feast of San Nicola, blessed on December 4 in the church and offered to the poor; the spiral-shaped loaf baked on December 13 in honor of Santa Lucia (protector of sight); the bread to commemorate the dead, symbolically molded into the shape of a pair of hands folded over a chest; and the breast-shaped bread to celebrate San Agata's day (protector of breasts).

Thanks to this tradition, bread became a blessed food and kneading, fermenting, cutting and cooking techniques have remained unchanged to this day, except that the wood-burning oven has been supplanted by... the electric one! Nonetheless, its taste and texture is still every bit as wonderful, especially when compared to the bread available on the peninsula. Without a doubt, the flour quality (*grano duro*) makes a huge difference where taste is concerned.

A staple food for Sicilians, bread is savored daily with *antipasti, pasta, pesce* and *carne.*

During the feast of Saint Joseph, the women and young girls in the village of Salemi, located in south-western Sicily, continue to follow tradition by sculpting bread dough into various shapes including shells, fish, and grape clusters. These works of art are baked and then set down on church altars.

Maria Zingarelli, a Sicilian at heart, really wanted us to taste the island bread. She also fed us arancinis, a caponata and a pasta con le sarde. Doused with white wine (Inzolia and Frappato di Cantina Valle dell'Acate) these dishes were quite simply exquisite and divine.

Pane di Maria
MARIA'S BREAD

SERVES 6 TO 8 (4 LOAVES)

2 lbs (1 kg) durum or all-purpose flour

2 tablespoons (30 ml) fresh yeast* (or 2 packets dried yeast)

1 tablespoon (15 ml) salt

2 cups (500 ml) hot water

5 tablespoons (75 ml) olive oil

4 tablespoons (60 ml) raw sesame seeds

* Fresh yeast is available in bakeries and gourmet food stores. It is preferable to use fresh over dry.

Put the flour in a large bowl. Hollow out the center and place the yeast and salt into the hollow. Mix the dough by gradually adding water to achieve a smooth texture. Add 2 tablespoons of olive oil and continue kneading the dough for a few more minutes. Divide the dough into 4 balls and roll each of these into a baguette shape. Make an incision in the middle of each baguette and sprinkle with flour. Cover with a thick cloth and leave for 2 hours in a warm, dry spot (in the oven, for example, but don't turn it on). Then, brush the 4 baguettes with the remaining olive oil and sprinkle with sesame seeds. Bake in a preheated oven at 450 °F (230 °C) on an oiled baking sheet for an hour or until the loaves are golden brown all over.

A truly unusual sandwich

The highly original *guastelle* is a popular food item sold in all of Palermo's open-air markets. Vendors take a sesame roll and fill it with boiled beef spleen and lard followed by *ricotta* and *caciocavallo*. Not for those of you with high cholesterol… but as far as *fast-foods* go, this sandwich is a lot tastier than our insipid, pre-fab burgers.

Angelo, a sfincione *vendor.*

A number of different pizzas are available in Sicily and throughout Italy. Invented by the nuns at the famous Palermo convent of Di San Vito, sfincione is a thick-crust pizza covered with tomato sauce and salami. Today, in the heart of the Vucciria (Palermo's oldest market) and Capo markets, food vendors are eager for us to taste their wares.

Created with leftover bread dough and a very popular item in Sicily, focaccia is a kind of flatbread covered with a spread made of fresh herbs such as basil or rosemary. It is delicious with a trickle of extra virgin olive oil. And of course there's calzone, pizza pockets stuffed with fish, sausage, pecorino, black olives... and oven-baked or sometimes fried.

Pizza
PIZZA DOUGH

Many options are available to the pizza lover with this basic recipe (you can also halve the ingredients if need be) and you can freely improvise with the toppings... Try fresh tomatoes, anchovies, red peppers, broccoli, cauliflower, black or green olives, goat cheese, shrimp, smoked salmon, capers, onions, etc. Eaten throughout the world, pizza has been labeled as a fast-food *but this doesn't really do it justice. When homemade with top quality ingredients it takes on a truly Italian dimension.*

YIELDS 4 CRUSTS

2 tablespoons (30 ml) fresh yeast* (or 2 packets dried yeast)

1 ⅓ cup (300 ml) lukewarm water

2 teaspoons (10 ml) sugar

1 ½ lb (700 g) all-purpose flour

3 tablespoons (45 ml) salt

5 tablespoons (75 ml) extra virgin olive oil

* Fresh yeast is available in bakeries or gourmet food stores. It is preferable to use fresh yeast over dry.

In a large bowl, combine the yeast, water and sugar and let stand for 5 minutes.

Add the flour, salt and olive oil.

Knead the dough until it becomes smooth. Cover with a cloth and let stand for 2 hours in a warm, dry area. The oven (unheated of course) is an ideal place. Separate the dough into four balls and dip them in flour.

Spread a dough ball by stretching it over an oiled pizza pan (preferably one with holes) and add the ingredients of your choice (tomato sauce, vegetables, salami, and cheese, for instance). Brush the dough's edges with olive oil. Place in a preheated oven (500 °F/260 °C) on the middle rack for about 20 minutes or until the crust is golden brown.

Pizza ai carciofi
ARTICHOKE PIZZA

SERVES 2 TO 4

1 ball pizza dough (see recipe on page 43)

2 tablespoons (30 ml) tomato sauce

8 artichoke hearts

½ cup (125 ml) grated mozzarella

Work the dough over an oiled pizza pan until it reaches the desired size. Brush on the tomato sauce, garnish with artichokes and sprinkle with mozzarella. Place in a preheated oven (500 °F/260 °C) for about 15 to 20 minutes or until the crust is golden brown. If you wish, serve the pizza with a trickle of extra virgin olive oil.

Owner of the Antica Focacceria San Francesco, located via A. Paternostro in Old Palermo, Vincenzo Conticello represents the 7th generation to run this popular restaurant established in 1834. In a retro setting, clients are served traditional Palermitan dishes. Sicily will soon be coming to a restaurant near you since Signor Conticello will be opening Antica Focacceria franchises in New York, Miami, Toronto and Paris. Most of the antipasti and dessert recipes in this book were created in his Palermo restaurant. Grazie mille Vincenzo!

Cheese
AN AGE OLD TRADITION

Sicily is not just the land of bread, olive oil, wine and seafood. The cheese there is absolutely superb as well! Its taste is rather like the Sicilian landscape: strong, rustic and sensual, a treat for those who know how to appreciate boldly flavored gastronomical delights.

Caciocavallo, whose name dates back to the era when this cheese was transported on horseback, is made with cow's milk in the same fashion as mozzarella. In order to give it that elastic quality, the curds are cooked at 115 °F (45 °C) in whey and then immersed several times in hot water. The resulting mixture is then kneaded by hand to form a gourd and hung by a rope to ripen. The ageing time is between 3 and 13 months. During this period, the cheese is cleaned and coated with oil so that the rind becomes smooth and light gold in color. When still young, *caciocavallo* is a mild cheese but as it ages it becomes increasingly sharp. It is mainly used grated.

A direct descendant of *caciocavallo*, *provolone* is fabricated the same way. Several versions of this cheese exist across Italy but in Sicily, they call it *ragusano*. It is brick-shaped and can weigh up to 26 lbs (12 kg). This cheese is mainly used grated as well.

Another variety of cheese is *pecorino*, which is made from sheep's milk and has a flavor that varies from culture to culture in the Mediterranean. Sicilian *pecorino* is hard and usually contains peppercorns or saffron. The curds are left to ripen for four months. This cheese is also intended for grating.

The "*crème de la crème*", of course, is *ricotta*, which is nothing like its commercial counterpart found in supermarkets. What a pleasure it is to eat this fresh cow's milk or sheep's milk cheese right on the premises where it was made. Manufactured from whey and twice cooked (hence the name *ricotta*), this cheese really can't be exported because is has to be eaten within two or three days of its being made. The taste varies from land to land according to the amount of rain that falls and the type of plants the animals consume. If you have the good fortune to go to Sicily one day, try this taste experience: take a slice of toast and spread it with ricotta, orange marmalade, a little honey, grilled almonds and a dash of rum. Smooth and divinely delicious, this concoction is even better when accompanied by a glass of sweet wine such as Passito di Pantelleria Ben Ryé, a dessert wine produced by Donnafugata winemakers and boldly nicknamed the Sicilian Sauternes!

There are many other varieties of Sicilian cheeses besides the ones described above, but the latter are the most commonly available kinds in our grocery stores and cheese shops.

Zuppa di grano duro e legumi
BEAN AND BARLEY SOUP

SERVES 4 TO 6

5 oz (150 g) dry white kidney beans*
(canned ones will do)

5 oz (150 g) dry red kidney beans* (canned ones will do)

4 oz (120 g) pork lard cut into small cubes

2 medium onions, finely chopped

1 carrot, finely chopped

2 celery stalks, finely chopped

9 oz (250 g) pearl barley

8 cups (2 liters) water

Sea salt and pepper

Parsley to taste

The evening before you make this recipe, soak the beans in a large pot of water.

Barley was apparently the first cereal to be cultivated in Sicily. Boiled in salted water, barley flour was the Mediterranean staple diet. Then came wheat. Sicilian soups are generally very thick and provide hearty sustenance on cold winter days.

The following day, drain and rinse the beans. Cook in unsalted water until tender. While the beans are cooking, fry the lard cubes in a large pot until they are golden brown. Add the onion, carrot and celery and brown for 3 minutes. Add the barley and 8 cups (2 liters) of water. Cook for one hour.

When the hour is nearly up, add the cooked beans (or the canned ones, rinsed). When done, add salt and pepper to taste, then the parsley.

* In this day and age of busy schedules, you can allow yourself to substitute cooked dry beans with canned ones (drained and rinsed). The taste isn't quite the same, but the soup will still have that unmistakable Sicilian flavor.

If you are pressed for time, don't hesitate to use canned white kidney beans and lentils (drained and rinsed) instead of the dry variety. The canned beans have less vitamin content, but a percentage of iron remains nonetheless.

Zuppa di verdure di montagna
GREEN VEGETABLE SOUP

SERVES 4 TO 6

5 oz (150 g) dry white kidney beans

8 cups (2 liters) water

7 oz (200 g) green beans, sliced

1 medium potato, cut into cubes

5 oz (150 g) dry brown lentil beans

½ cup (125 ml) peas, fresh or frozen

1 cup (250 ml) fresh broccoli, sliced

1 cup (250 ml) fresh spinach, finely sliced

Fresh herbs to taste

Soak the white kidney beans overnight in water.

The following day, drain and rinse the beans. Cook them in unsalted water until tender.

When the beans are nearly done, boil 8 cups (2 liters) water. Add the green beans and potatoes. After 15 minutes, add the lentils, drained white kidney beans, peas, broccoli and spinach. Cook for 5 to 10 minutes. When done, add salt and pepper to taste as well as any fresh herbs you wish.

Insalata di arance e finocchio
ORANGE AND FENNEL SALAD

A fresh, aromatic salad that is perfect as an appetizer, especially when followed by a main course of fish or meat.

SERVES 4

1 bulb fennel root

1 medium red onion

3 oranges (preferably blood oranges)

4 tablespoons (60 ml) extra virgin olive oil

Sea salt and pepper to taste

Carve up the fennel, onion and the oranges any way you like. Add the olive oil, salt and pepper and mix.

Available in our food stores in fall and winter, fennel should be firm in texture.

Sweet, ruby tinted blood oranges are as pleasing to the eye as they are to the palate. They are available in our food stores mostly in January, February and March.

Salvatore Simoncini presented us with this truly classic Sicilian dish, also very popular in the Italian coastal provinces. Seafood is the house specialty at the Calogero restaurant in Mondello. It is served as a salad or with pasta on beautiful plates created by reputed Sicilian ceramist Nino Parrucci.

Insalata di frutti di mare
SEAFOOD SALAD

SERVES 6

10 oz (300 g) octopus, cut into ½ inch (1 cm) pieces

7 oz (200 g) squid

1 lb (450 g) mussels, washed

10 oz (300 g) shrimp

2 celery stalks, thinly sliced

½ cup (125 ml) olive oil

Juice of 2 lemons

Parsley

Boil the octopus for about 6 minutes in salted water with a slice of lemon. When the pieces are tender, drain and set aside. Do the same with the squid. Cook the mussels in a frying pan and remove from the heat once they open.

Shell the mussels and set aside.

Boil 8 cups (2 liters) salted water, drop in the shrimp and immediately remove the pot from the stove. It takes just a few minutes for the shrimp to cook (become pink and curled-up). Let them cool and then shell them.

Mix the seafood on a platter, add the celery and season with olive oil, lemon and parsley. Add salt and pepper to taste.

Sea salt
SICILY'S WHITE GOLD

Nicknamed "white gold" in Sicily, salt is often seen as an enemy to our health when it is in fact a completely natural element, every bit as vital to our systems as is water, in addition to being a natural component of the human body.

The common belief is that salt, even when used in reasonable amounts, is a health-threatening substance causing water retention, cellulite, and, by extension, obesity.

There are two types of salt: rock salt and sea salt. Nowadays, the most popular form of this mineral is rock salt that comes from sedimentary rock and is commonly found on most grocery store shelves and at most restaurant tables. This industrial type of salt is sterilized, pasteurized and then supplemented with iodine. It is suitable enough for cooking food in water and is used in both the food and chemical industries.

Sea salt, a pure substance, is a superior product because it has not been subjected to any chemical changes and it contains trace elements that are excellent for your health. Contrary to rock salt, it won't bloat you or make you fat; it will in fact contribute to your overall health in a natural way.

Thanks to gourmets during the last decade, sea salt has regained its merit. Coarse salt is ideal for marinades, soups and pickled meats. As for fine salts, they add fla-

Rebuilt 500 years ago, the Marsala and Trapani salt works have been around since the Phoenicians' arrival in the VIIIth century BC. A water mill pushes the high tide into the numerous salt basins. The sun's heat causes the water to evaporate and pure salt to form, after which it is stacked into pyramids and left to dry for a year.

vor to appetizers, salads, meat and fish. But the *nec plus ultra* is a flower of salt which is in high demand. It has been sold for several years now on the international markets. The salt is collected near the surface of windswept saltpans. An exceptionally sophisticated product, it has some truly unique taste nuances. It isn't meant for cooking since it is fine enough to become volatile.

The quest for salt throughout the ages has often resulted in the thirst for conquest. Today, it is a vital ingredient to our diet.

PROPERTIES OF SALT

We've known for a long time now about salt's ability to preserve foods such as cooked meats, fish and cheese. To better protect the mineral from humidity, it's a good idea to drop a few grains of rice into the saltcellar. The health benefits of salt include its power to relax you when added to the bath water and its power to prevent inflammation when applied to a wound with a saturated cloth. Copper pots scrubbed with lemon and fine salt will have greater luster and cut flowers will stay fresh longer when a pinch of salt is added to the water.

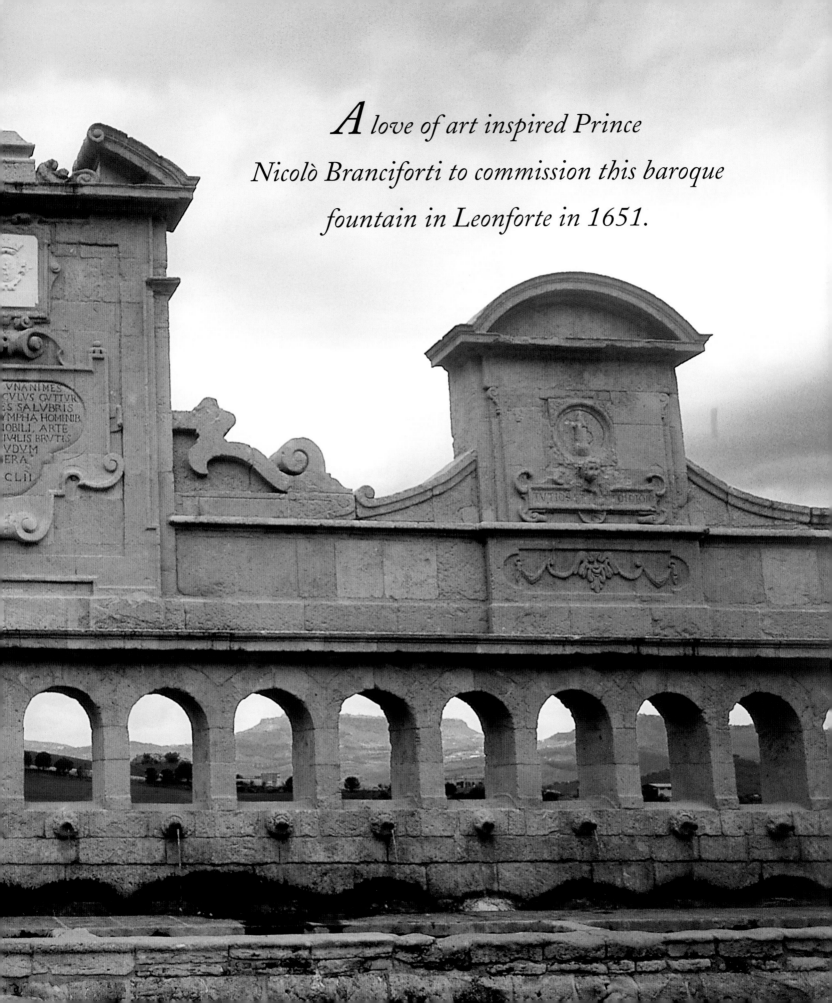

A love of art inspired Prince Nicolò Branciforti to commission this baroque fountain in Leonforte in 1651.

BASIC TOMATO SAUCE

YIELDS 750 ML TO 1 LITER

4 tablespoons (60 ml) extra virgin olive oil

1 onion, finely sliced

1 clove garlic, finely chopped

2 lbs (1 kg) well-ripened Italian tomatoes, coarsely chopped

1 tablespoon (15 ml) sea salt

1 tablespoon (15 ml) honey or cane sugar

½ tablespoon (7.5 ml) oregano

Pour the olive oil into a saucepan and brown the onion and garlic for two minutes. Add the tomatoes, salt, honey and oregano. Cook for 30 to 45 minutes over low heat, stirring occasionally. Process the sauce through a vegetable mill.

If fresh Italian tomatoes are not available in your food stores, use 1 lb (450 g) of canned Italian tomatoes as a substitute. That fresh tomato taste will of course be missing but you can still obtain a rich and flavorful sauce.

The secret of pasta *al dente*

Should you ever visit Sicily, you'll notice that Sicilians, contrary to Northern Italians, adore eating pasta *al dente*. There's a simple reason for this: the islanders love the feeling of firm pasta between their teeth.

As much as possible chose durum semolina pasta, which is made with superior quality flour.

For 4 to 6 portions, boil 5 quarts (5 liters) of water with 4 tablespoons (60 ml) of salt. Slide 1 lb (500 g) pasta into the boiling water and cook according to directions on the package. When done, pour a ladle of cold water into the pot to stop further cooking. Drain and rinse the pasta.

Dried Tomatoes

Imported from Mexico in the XVIth century by Spanish sailors, the tomato is omnipresent in Sicilian cooking. In addition to sauces and pastas, Sicily also produces a lot of sun-dried tomatoes. The country's sun-drenched climate is ideal for sun-dried tomatoes whilst in Nordic climates we must be content with oven-drying.

Choose well-ripened tomatoes of the San Marzano or Romanella variety. Cut them lengthwise in two and salt the tops (use sea salt). Place them on a baking sheet and put them in the oven (the oven door must remain slightly ajar) heated between 175 °F and 200 °F (80 °C and 100 °C) for 8 to 12 hours. Preserve the dried tomatoes in olive oil with oregano or basil, chili peppers and bay leaves. They make delicious antipasti and add zest to the pasta of your choice.

Spaghetti con pomodoro, melanzane, peperoni e capperi
PASTA WITH TOMATOES, EGGPLANT, PEPPERS AND CAPERS

SERVES 4 TO 6

1 lb (500 g) spaghetti

1 onion, finely chopped

1 red pepper, finely chopped

10 well-ripened Italian tomatoes cut into large chunks

½ cup (125 ml) white wine

1 medium eggplant cut into large chunks

3 tablespoons (45 ml) capers

Salt and pepper

Olive oil

Brown the onion in olive oil, and add the red pepper, tomatoes and capers. Cook for 10 minutes, then, deglaze the mixture with white wine.

Brown the eggplant in another frying pan. Add it to the above mixture. Cook the pasta (see page 58). Pour the sauce over the pasta.

Eggplant is a highly valued ingredient in Sicilian cooking. So are capers. Apparently, the best ones come from the volcanic Pantelleria Island located off Sicily's west coast. In the Eolian archipelago, north of Sicily, Salina Island is also known for its capers. Preserved in rock salt, capers should be soaked in fresh water for 15 minutes before use.

Pasta al Ragù
PASTA WITH MEAT SAUCE

SERVES 4 TO 6

1 lb (500 g) maccheroni

2 tablespoons (30 ml) extra virgin olive oil

14 oz (400 g) ground beef or veal

1 onion, finely chopped

3 garlic cloves, finely sliced

1 carrot, sliced

1 celery stalk, diced

¾ cup (180 ml) white wine

1 ⅓ lb (600 g) fresh or canned Italian tomatoes

2 bay leaves

½ tablespoon (7.5 ml) oregano

Salt and pepper to taste

In a saucepan, brown the ground beef, onion, garlic, carrots and celery in 2 tablespoons olive oil for 10 minutes. Add the wine and let it evaporate. Then, add the tomatoes and bay leaves. Salt and pepper to taste. Allow the sauce to simmer for one hour. Add the oregano last. Cook the *maccheroni al dente* (see page 58), and when the pasta is done and drained, pour a ladle full (or more!) of meat sauce on each portion. Garnish with basil.

This classic pasta dish prepared by Peppé Giuffré, renowned chef and owner of Giardino Eden, via Pitagora, in Trapani, and a caterer in Palermo, was highly appreciated by our production crew between two photo shoots. Peppé generously provided us with a number of the wonderful concoctions in this book, including recipes for soup, fish and meat. Grazie mille Peppé!

Many versions of this recipe can be found
on the island and throughout Italy.

Maccheroni alla Norma
NORMA'S PASTA

A typical dish created by a Catania restaurant owner in honor of Bellini's opera Norma, *who was a native of the east coast Sicilian city.*

SERVES 4 TO 6

1 lb (500 g) maccheroni or bucatini pasta*

1 onion, finely chopped

8 tablespoons (120 ml) extra virgin olive oil

10 fresh Italian tomatoes, peeled

4 tablespoons (60 ml) basil, minced

2 eggplants, cut into large chunks

4 oz (120 g) fresh ricotta

* Real maccheroni *is cylindrical in shape and is not like the macaroni we find in our grocery stores here.* Bucatini *are very wide spaghetti.*

Cook the pasta (see page 58). In the meantime, brown the onion in 2 tablespoons of olive oil. Add the tomatoes and cook for about 20 minutes until the sauce is thick. Pour this mixture into another container.

In the same frying pan used for the tomatoes and onions, fry the eggplant in the remaining olive oil until it is golden brown. If you need to use more olive oil that's fine; eggplant absorbs fat very quickly. Add the fried eggplant to the tomato sauce. Pour this sauce over the pasta and add some fresh *ricotta*.

You might want to reserve a few eggplant chunks to decorate your dish.

If the tomato sauce is acidic, you can mellow the taste by adding some cane sugar or honey from mixed blossoms, which will give it a more traditional (and delicious!) taste.

Pasta con le sarde
PASTA WITH SARDINES

Since wild fennel is hard to find, you can replace it with dill. Dill certainly doesn't have the same taste as fennel but is definitely the next best thing. In Italian grocery stores or fish markets, you can buy a box of condimenti con le sarde *that contains wild fennel and tastes close enough to the real thing.*

SERVES 4 TO 6

*7 oz (200 g) wild fennel
(or 2 bunches fresh dill)*

14 oz (400 g) or 8 fresh sardines

1 tablespoon (15 ml) salt

1 medium onion, finely chopped

2 tablespoons (30 ml) olive oil

½ teaspoon (2.5 ml) salt

2 salted anchovies

1 ½ tablespoons (22.5 ml) pine nuts

1 tablespoon (15 ml) currants

Hot water

2 cups (500 ml) tomato sauce*

1 lb (500 g) bucatini

6 tablespoons (90 ml) breadcrumbs

* In the Enna region, in Leonforte, tomato sauce is added to the pasta con le sarde. *This tones down the fish flavor and makes for a smoother sauce.*

Cook the wild fennel or bunches of dill (don't forget to remove the roots and rinse) in lightly salted boiling water for 15 minutes.

During this time, first chop off the heads and tails, then remove the fins and fillet the sardines. Next, sweat the onion in 2 tablespoons of olive oil. Add the fennel or dill (coarsely shredded), sardines and salt, and cook for 5 minutes over medium heat, stirring lightly to shred the sardines. Add the anchovies, pine nuts and currants (previously soaked in hot water) and continue cooking for 10 minutes, mixing carefully. If you decide to add tomato sauce to this mixture, cook for an additional 30 minutes.

While the *bucatini* are cooking in salted water, brown the breadcrumbs. Combine the pasta and sauce. Sprinkle with the fried breadcrumbs.

Pasta con le sarde is a popular dish originating from the city of Palermo.

Penne con ricotta e pistacchi
PASTA WITH RICOTTA AND PISTACHIOS

Easy to make, even at the last minute, this recipe is appreciated not only for its taste but also for its color scheme. If you can get hold of edible flowers, do use them to decorate your dishes.

SERVES 4 TO 6

1 lb (500 g) penne

Sea salt and pepper

1 lb (500 g) fresh ricotta

½ cup (125 ml) cooking water (pasta)

½ cup (125 ml) salted pistachios, finely chopped

Olive oil

Cook the pasta *al dente* in salted water (see page 58). Drain the pasta but reserve ½ cup (125 ml) of cooking water. Mix the salt and pepper with the *ricotta* and add the cooking water to soften the mixture. Combine the *ricotta* with the pasta. Garnish with the pistachios and a trickle of olive oil.

The ricotta *available in our grocery stores is a more commercial variety than what is produced in Italy where ricotta is homemade and must be eaten within 3 days of fabrication. Outside of Italy, you can find home made* ricotta, *but for freshness and refinement, it will never come close to Italian* ricotta.

Pasta con le zucchine
PASTA WITH ZUCCHINI

This quick and easy dish has definite vegetarian appeal. So does another popular Sicilian pasta dish made with cauliflower, pine nuts, raisins, anchovies and pecorino (goat's cheese). Unfortunately, we were unable to produce this recipe because no cauliflower was available in the Palermo markets in May. This is a wonderful example of the Sicilian way of life where fresh produce, available only in season, is local and not imported.

SERVES 4 TO 6

1 lb (500 g) spaghetti

8 tablespoons (120 ml) extra virgin olive oil

4 cloves garlic, minced

4 green or yellow zucchinis cut into thin slices

Sea salt and pepper to taste

Ricotta salata*, pecorino or parmigiano reggiano

While the pasta is cooking (see page 58), use a non-stick frying pan to brown the garlic in olive oil. Remove it from the pan. Add the zucchini and brown the slices on each side. Reserve.

Drain the pasta and serve it on plates. Distribute the zucchini slices on each portion. Trickle 1 tablespoon extra virgin olive oil and grate some *ricotta salata, pecorino* or *parmigiano reggiano* over the servings.

*Ricotta salata is a hard, salted Sicilian cheese made from either cow's or sheep's milk that is becoming increasingly available in Italian grocery stores or specialized cheese shops.

Pasta alla Magda
MAGDA'S PASTA

Magda's pasta is the Artistic Director's (photo) creation, inspired in part from a typical Palermitan recipe. Extra tasty and inexpensive too!

SERVES 4 TO 6

1 lb (500 g) bucatini

5 tablespoons (75 ml) extra virgin olive oil

1 garlic clove, minced

1 mild red pepper, finely chopped (or ½ chili pepper, finely sliced)

12 kalamata black olives, pitted and diced

4 tablespoons (60 ml) breadcrumbs

While the pasta is cooking in salted water (see page 58), sauté the garlic in a non-stick pan in 3 tablespoons (45 ml) of olive oil. Once it has browned, remove it from the frying pan. Add the red pepper (or chili pepper) and brown for 5 minutes. Add the olives, cook for an additional 3 minutes and set aside.

In a small frying pan, brown the breadcrumbs in the remaining olive oil. Once the pasta is cooked, combine it with the red pepper and olive mixture. Serve the pasta and sprinkle each plate with the fried breadcrumbs. For extra deliciousness, trickle some extra virgin olive oil over your pasta.

Avoid commercial breadcrumbs, as they often taste of cardboard. Homemade breadcrumbs are very easy to make. Simply grate finely some dry bread, preferably a baguette.

Pasta con lenticchie alla Palermitana
PALERMITAN PASTA
WITH LENTILS

SERVES 4 TO 6

Lentils are usually used in soups but are delicious in a pasta recipe such as this one.

1 lb (500 g) pasta of your choice

7 oz (200 g) brown lentils

1 onion, finely chopped

1 chili pepper, finely chopped

2 tablespoons (30 ml) olive oil

1 to 1 ¼ cup (250 to 300 ml) water

Sea salt and pepper to taste

Pecorino

In a frying pan, brown the onion and chili pepper in olive oil. Add the lentils and cook for 3 minutes to blend the flavors. Add water to this mixture. Cook over very low heat until the lentils are no longer crunchy. If necessary, add some more water. Cook the pasta (see page 58). Pour the lentil mixture over the pasta. Salt, pepper and serve with a trickle of olive oil. Sprinkle *pecorino* cheese to taste.

Spaghetti ai gamberetti
PASTA WITH SHRIMP

In northern Sicily, as you near the Eolian Islands, you'll encounter a number of shrimp-based recipes. According to Sicilian culinary history, pasta with shrimp was never a popular dish since only the aristocracy could afford it.

SERVES 4 TO 6

1 lb (500 g) spaghetti

2 celery stalks, finely chopped

1 onion, finely chopped

½ cup (125 ml) white wine

1 lb (500 g) fresh shrimp (preferably gray), shelled

2 tomatoes, peeled and cut into large chunks

1 clove garlic, minced

1 tablespoon (15 ml) chili peppers

2 tablespoons (30 ml) extra virgin olive oil

While the spaghetti is cooking (see page 58), cook the celery and onion with the white wine in a cast iron cooking pot over low heat. Once the wine has evaporated, add the shrimp, tomatoes, garlic, chili peppers and olive oil. Cover the pot and cook for just a few minutes. Avoid prolonged cooking, as this will toughen the shrimp. When the pasta is ready, drain and mix with the sauce.

Risotto alla siciliana
SICILIAN RICE

SERVES 4

12 oz (350 g) rice (carnaroli, nano vialone or arborio)*

1 medium red onion, finely chopped

2 peppers, preferably red or yellow, cut into squares

1 eggplant, cut into cubes

7 oz (200 g) red tomatoes, peeled and cubed

2 squids, sliced into rings

28 oz (800 g) fish fillet (cod, haddock or grouper) cut into large chunks

14 oz (400 g) medium shrimps, shelled

6 tablespoons (90 ml) white wine

2 cups (500 ml) fish broth (see page 82)

Basil

* Small and round, this type of rice is available in Italian grocery stores and supermarkets.

Cook the rice *al dente* (i.e. crunchy) in salted water. Drain and set aside.

In a large frying pan, brown the following ingredients separately in the following order: onion and garlic, peppers, eggplant and tomatoes. Set aside. In another frying pan, sauté the squid, fish and shrimp one at a time. Deglaze the pan with white wine. Add the fish broth. Cook for a few minutes. Next, add the rice, vegetables and fish and allow to cook for 5 minutes. For moister rice, add more fish broth.

Sprinkle with parsley and decorate with basil leaves before serving.

Risotto is a dish stemming from the north of Italy but the Sicilians were quick to adopt it since rice is both nourishing and inexpensive. This particular recipe exudes the delicious sea aromas of Sicily.

Olive Oil
A TASTE OF SICILIAN GOLD

An industry originally started in Asia Minor, olive growing in Sicily began in the VIIIth century BC. This is truly one of Greece's greatest gifts to Sicily because to this day the olive tree remains an inexhaustible source of life giving nourishment.

A LITTLE HISTORY

According to Greek mythology, several legends refer to the olive tree. One of the best known tells the story of an argument between Athena (precious daughter of Zeus, King of the Gods) and Poseidon (God of the Sea) over which one of them had the right to build a temple on the Acropolis. Zeus intervened by proposing a contest whereby the winner would gain the right to build the temple by offering humanity the most useful life-giving gift. Poseidon came up with the horse while Athena created the olive tree. The gift of a tree that provided both light and nourishment earned the goddess her victory. Athena set out to have her temple built on the Acropolis. This structure was named the Parthenon, a Greek term related to virginity.

A DYNAMIC INDUSTRY

With several microclimates favorable to olive growing, Sicily now has more than 180,000 hectares of olive groves. Next to Puglia and Calabrio, Sicily is the third largest olive oil producer in Italy with an annual output totaling more than 11 million gallons (50 million liters). Although it is spread all over Sicily, the highest concentration of olive oil production is in the Trapani, Belice Valley, Agrigento and Ragusa regions. Thanks to better harvesting methods, more modern equipment and greater concern for quality, Sicilian olive oil started to gain the recognition it deserved about five years ago. Three of these oils are part of the DOP (an acronym referring to a guarantee of quality control): Monti Iblei, Valli Trapanesi and Val di Mazara.

The most common olives in Sicily are indigenous ones, which means that Sicilian olive oils have their very own unique taste in comparison with other Mediterranean products. Amongst some of the most frequently harvested varieties, the Biancolilla, the Nocellarea del Belice, the Nocellarea Etnea, the Ogliarola and the Santagatese.

Sicilian olive oil is characterized by its intense, almost golden yellow color, its mid-range density and a fruity flavor that veers between medium and strong. Many subtle flavors can be detected in the aftertaste including nuances of red or green tomatoes, hints of almond and artichoke, all melding together into a crescendo of exquisite taste.

Natalia Ravida, a Memfi olive grower, is proud of her 300-year-old olive tree.

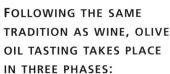

FOLLOWING THE SAME TRADITION AS WINE, OLIVE OIL TASTING TAKES PLACE IN THREE PHASES:

Color: by analyzing the oil's color, you can determine whether a particular product is cloudy or clear. There is, however, no link between color and quality.

Bouquet: This is a very important step because it allows the taster to detect not only any fragrance flaws, but also the bouquet's particular qualities or intensity.

Taste: At this stage, the oil's degree of bitterness or sweetness can be assessed. Bitterness is felt at the back of the throat, while sweetness is detected on the tongue. During this phase of taste testing, it is possible to highlight other positive flavor nuances such as hints of artichoke, tomato or almond. Conversely, negative flavor traits can be discerned such as rancidity, moldiness or a taste of sediment.

Don't confuse acidity with sharpness since the latter attribute is a natural outcome that depends on the quantity of polyphenols (a chemical component of the olive) contained in the oil. The taste test finale is important since it allows you to evaluate flavor duration.

HOW TASTING IS DONE

Fill a teaspoon with 3 ml (approximately ½ teaspoon) of oil and place it in your mouth. Use your tongue to

74   *Sicily: A way of life*

circulate the oil. At this point, you inhale a puff of air so that the combination of heat and oxygen will bring out the particular flavors and aromas of the oil. Following this, slightly masticate and then simply swallow the oil, which is excellent for the digestion.

CHOOSING A GOOD QUALITY OLIVE OIL
Even if the consumer recognizes the benefits of olive oil, making the right selection can be tricky.

It is preferable to buy olive oil in an opaque glass bottle, which does not allow any light to filter through and alter the taste. It is essential that the label bear the mention "extra virgin". Also make sure that there is a visible expiry date as well as an attestation as to the country of origin. High quality oil contains a very low level of acidity (under 1%) and has a shelf life of 12 to 24 months after bottling. Quality is not a question of price but the guarantee that quality control is present, which is indicated by the letters DOP or HS.

Natalia's recipe

SERVES 4

14 oz (400 g) short pasta, such as pennete

7 oz (200 g) green olives, pitted

1 garlic clove

4 to 6 fl oz (125 to 175 ml) extra virgin olive oil

1 ½ teaspoons (7.5 ml) capers, desalted and rinsed

1 pinch chili peppers

Sea salt to taste

Mint leaves or parsley to decorate

Put all the ingredients through a mixer until you obtain a smooth creamy paste. You can conserve this sauce in a glass container by simply adding a layer of olive oil over the mixture.

Once the pasta is ready, set a little of the cooking water aside to dilute the sauce as needed. Combine the pasta and sauce and garnish with a trickle of olive oil, a few tomato slices and some other vegetables of your choice. Sprinkle with finely chopped mint or parsley leaves.

Contemporary Sicily is slowly waking up to the rest of the modern world. In spite of today's tendency for cultures to speedily assimilate each other, the Sicilian way of life remains happily intact. So unique is this particular culture, one feels like telling the islanders: "Don't ever change a thing!"

Tonno al forno con pomodori ed olio di oliva
BAKED TUNA WITH TOMATOES AND OLIVE OIL

God bless Poseidon or Neptune, for the sea off the coast of Trapani is not polluted. That's where, for centuries now, fishermen have been practicing the tonnara, *traditional tuna fishing. A few kilometers from the shore, huge nets designed to catch these giants of the sea are tossed from the fishing boats into the ocean. Once the tuna is trapped in the net, fishermen use harpoons to finish it off. It's an impressive spectacle. Even if 75% of the catch is sold to Japan, there is still enough fish left to satisfy the hearty appetites of* trattorie *or* ristorante *patrons on the isle.*

Favor red tuna over yellow because it is tastier.

SERVES 4

19 oz (540 g) tuna or 4 slices tuna (1 in./2 cm thick)

2 lemons, sliced

10 bay leaves

2 garlic cloves, minced

½ cup (125 ml) extra virgin olive oil

2 oz (60 g) almonds, chopped

1 ½ cup (375 ml) tomato sauce or 3 fresh, sliced tomatoes

Zest from 2 lemons

¾ cup (180 ml) white wine

2 stalks fresh mint

Place the tuna in an oiled oven dish. Add the lemon slices, bay leaves and minced garlic cloves.

Pour olive oil over the whole thing. Make a few cuts in the tuna to insert the mint leaves and almonds. Cover the tuna with tomato sauce or tomato slices and place in an oven preheated at 360 °F (180 °C) for 20 minutes. Douse from time to time with white wine.

Pesce spada con limone
LEMON SWORDFISH

SERVES 4

4 swordfish steaks, 7 oz (200 g) each

15 bay leaves

2 lemons, sliced

½ cup (125 ml) extra virgin olive oil

Sea salt and pepper to taste

2 onions, finely chopped

½ cup (125 ml) almonds, slivered

Zest from 2 lemons

¾ cup (180 ml) white wine

2 tablespoons (30 ml) parsley

In an oiled oven dish, intersperse the bay leaves and lemon slices to form a circle. Cover with olive oil and arrange the swordfish steaks overtop. Season with salt and pepper. Place a portion of chopped onion over each fish steak and cover the whole with a mixture of almonds and lemon zest. Place in a pre-heated oven (400 °F/200 °C) for 20 minutes. Halfway through cooking time, douse the swordfish with white wine. Garnish with parsley and serve.

Mamone Cosimo, a Mondello fisherman, presented us with this swordfish dish.

Baccalà alla ghiotta
SUMPTUOUS COD

SERVES 4

1 ⅓ lb (600 g) salted cod or
4 fresh cod fillets

1 onion, finely chopped

4 fresh tomatoes, sliced

3 tablespoons (45 ml) currants

¾ cup (180 ml) green olives, pitted
and chopped

1 tablespoon (15 ml) capers

Zest from 2 lemons

½ cup (125 ml) olive oil

4 tablespoons (60 ml) dry white wine

If the recipe is made with dried cod, you will have to soak it 12 hours in cold water beforehand and change the water at least 4 times.

In an oiled oven dish, place half the tomatoes and onions and all of the fish. Add the rest of the tomatoes and onions, the currants, olives, capers and the zest of two lemons. Pour on the olive oil and white wine.

Bake in a preheated oven (450 °F/230 °C) for 20 minutes.

Filetti di orata all'arancia
PIKE FILLETS WITH ORANGE SAUCE

SERVES 4

4 pike fillets (about 4 oz/125 g each)

1 quart (1 liter) fish broth

3 tablespoons (80 g) butter

¼ cup (60 ml) flour

3 oz (90 ml) freshly squeezed orange juice

1 orange, peeled and cut into pieces

Zest from 1 orange

Bring the fish broth to a boil in a large, shallow cooking pot and immerse the fillets. Remove the fillets after 5 minutes and keep them warm. Melt the butter in a frying pan and add the flour, stirring continuously until you get a smooth paste. Slowly add the fish broth, orange juice and orange pieces, using a rapid whisk movement until you get a smooth, velvety texture. Place the fish fillets on lettuce leaves and pour on the fish broth and orange sauce. Decorate with orange zest

Fish broth

MAKES ABOUT 1 GALLON (4 ½) LITERS

2 lbs (1 kg) fish carcasses

1 onion, cut into quarters

1 celery stalk, coarsely chopped

1 carrot, sliced

3 bay leaves

5 quarts (5 liters) water

Salt and pepper

Ask your fishmonger for carcasses to make fish broth. All you have to do is place all the ingredients in a cast iron pot and cook over low heat for 1 to 3 hours. Then, strain the mixture. It can be kept for about 5 days in the refrigerator.

Calamari alla Siciliana
SICILIAN SQUID

SERVES 4

6 large squids with tentacles

1 onion, finely chopped

5 cloves garlic, minced

4 ripe tomatoes, diced

¾ cup (180 ml) white wine

¾ cup (180 ml) black olives, pitted and finely chopped

4 tablespoons (60 ml) capers

1 tablespoon (15 ml) fresh basil

Ask your fishmonger to clean the squid. If you have to do it yourself, remove the ink sacks and then cut the squid into rings. Brown the onion and garlic. Add the squid rings and diced tomatoes. Cook for 5 minutes over low heat, gradually adding the white wine, pitted black olives, capers and basil. Cook for another 5 minutes over low heat and serve.

Cuscus con pesce
FISH COUSCOUS

If you don't have a couscous maker (pressure cooker for cooking durum semolina), here is the simplest way to proceed: boil 4 cups (1 liter) of water with 2 tablespoons (30 ml) of olive oil. In the meantime, put the semolina in a large bowl. When the water has boiled, gradually add it to the couscous so that the latter will absorb it. Add a little olive oil and use a fork to break up any clumps in the semolina.

In a large frying pan, brown the onion, garlic, celery and tomatoes in olive oil. Add the fish, cinnamon clove and parsley. Add 8 cups (2 liters) boiling water and cook for one hour. If you want, you can reduce this fish sauce with a mixer or serve it directly on a bed of couscous.

Legend has it that couscous was brought to Africa by Moses and Jacob during their peregrinations. Thanks to commercial exchanges and immigration, this dish rapidly gained popularity. In Morocco and Algeria, meat is an essential ingredient, while in Tunisia and Sicily, couscous is given a Mediterranean touch with fish. This is a typical dish in the city of Trapani and dates back to the XVth century.

SERVES 4 TO 6

2 lbs (1 kg) durum semolina

4 cups (1 liter) water

2 tablespoons (30 ml) extra virgin olive oil

6 tablespoons (90 ml) extra virgin olive oil

1 onion, finely chopped

3 cloves garlic, minced

1 celery stalk, finely chopped

5 tomatoes, peeled and diced

3 lbs (1 ½ kg) white fish (suitable for soup) cut into large chunks

½ teaspoon (2.5 ml) cinnamon

1 clove

Parsley

8 cups (2 liters) boiling water

Sea salt and pepper to taste

Sicily's
WINE BOOM

The art of winemaking in Sicily is nothing new. According to archaeological findings, the Phoenicians from the VIIIth century BC would have been the first to take up the trade. It was only during the XIVth century that viticulture became such a rapidly expanding industry. So much so that huge quantities were being exported to Northern Italy. But in spite of the increase in production, the quality of the wine often left something to be desired. Today, thanks to young wine makers who have been schooled in the art, trade with other wine producing countries and a greater access to better equipment, the quality of Sicilian wine is on the rise. Sicilian viticulture — with red wine gaining popularity on the island over the formerly more sought after white — is becoming more and more sophisticated, in addition to carving itself a niche on the international market. Because of this, the DOC Siciliana (*denominazione di origine controllata*) was created a few years ago to ensure a standard of quality control. Only 2% of Sicilian wines bear this label: Alcamo DOC, Cerasuolo di Vittoria DOC, Contessa Entellina DOC, Etna Rosso DOC, Faro DOC, Malvasia delle Lipari DOC, Marsala DOC, Moscato di Noto DOC, and Moscato di Pantelleria Passito DOC.

With 200,000 available hectares, Sicily's annual wine output is over 240 million gallons (11 million hectoliters), 50% of which comes from the province of Alcamo on the north-western side of the island. Northern Italian wine producers are becoming positively passionate about Sicilian viticulture, going so far as to establish partnerships with the island's wine makers or even acquiring vineyards in Sicily. The island's climatic conditions (torrid summers, weak precipitation) and the poor quality of the soil are now viewed as assets rather than obstacles. These facts, combined with Sicilian pride in homegrown products, make the island a very favorable and dynamic location for viticulture.

INTERNATIONAL PRODUCERS

Concern for quality and better processing of juice from the grape have pushed Sicily's wines into a greater international prominence. On the international, as well as on the local front, there are a few wine-makers who really stand out.

Duca di Salaparuta, one of Sicily's oldest wine merchants, produces classic wines such as white and red Corvo, a Brut Riserva (restricted output), Colomba Platino, a fresh and fruity white, Terra d'Agala, a subtle red wine, the elegant Duca Enrico and Ala, a fortified wine.

Between the provinces of Palermo and Agrigento, the Tasca d'Almerita family produce a small collection of white wines, among them a divinely fruity, slightly woody Chardonnay, the elegantly structured Nozze

d'Oro, the pleasingly dry Regaleali Bianco, and the raspberry nuanced Regaleali Rosato. They also offer some red wines, notably the rich and full-bodied Rosso del Conte and Regaleali Rosso, a red with delightfully lingering aromas.

In Vittoria, the Azienda Agricola Cos produces Cerasuolo, a hardy, rustic wine typical of the region.

The Carlo Pellegrino winery in Marsala offers memorable dessert wines such as the subtle, delicate Moscato di Pantelleria and Passito di Pantelleria with its apricot aromas.

Also in Marsala, the Donnafugata family creates an excellent, dry, slightly vanilla-flavored white, Chiaranda del merlo, and Il Rosso di Donnafugata, a wine with a rich, red fruit aroma which is slightly tannic.

Last but not least, De Bartoli, the ultimate Marsala promoter, offers fortified wines such as Vecchio Samperi (10 years of age) with its dried fruit bouquet, Marsala Superiore (10 years of age) with hints of cocoa and

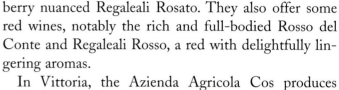

From left to right: the Donnafugata family in Marsala; a vineyard owned by the Firriato wine merchants in Trapani; the Planeta family in Agrigento.

From left to right:
Lilly Fazio; baby Alfredo
Donnafugata.
Below: Francesco Spadafora.
Right page: The grape
harvest at Tasca d'Almerita.

Bukkuram Moscato di Pantelleria, a dessert wine with a pleasing honey aroma aftertaste.

In the Caltanisetta region, the Averna group has distinguished itself with Amaro Siciliano, a digestive liqueur developed from natural herbs which is gaining popularity in America.

On the list of highly skilled young producers is the Planeta family who offers a mellow and woody Chardonnay, a Merlot, as well as an excellent, world-class Cabernet-Sauvignon.

In the province of Ragusa, young Gaetana Iacono produces an Inzolia-Chardonnay blend, a full-bodied Cerasuolo di Vittoria, and Frappato, a light red wine that is served chilled.

In Trapani, the Fazio family is representative of the new generation of wine makers. They produce 10 wines including a delightfully fresh Inzolia, the cherry-nuanced Nero d'Avola and Müller Thurgau, a sweet wine with a hint of mandarin.

Since 1995, the Firriato wine merchants, headed by brothers Salvatore and Girolamo di Gaetano, have had an annual output of 4 million bottles. Sold all over the world, these wines have a distinctively Sicilian taste. Among the wines developed by these merchants: the Primula, Santa Gostino, Alcamo, Altavilla whites and the Etna Rosso red.

Located 60 kilometres south of Palermo, Virzi has an inspiring vineyard owned by Francesco Spadafora. This dynamic wine grower has developed eight very distinguished wines including the aromatic white Di Vino, the Don Pietro red with a hint of raspberry, and Schietto, a Cabernet-Sauvignon bursting with heady fruit flavor. A remarkably skilled wine grower, Francesco Spadafora always places the emphasis on quality before quantity.

The Main Sicilian Vines

The main vines used for creating white wines are the Inzolia, the Cataratto, the Grillo and the Malvasia, and for the reds, the primary vines employed are the Nero d'avola, the Nerello mascalese, the Perricone and the Frappato di Vittoria. With these indigenous vines, a number of successful blends are created in combination with world-class vines such as Chardonnay, Sauvignon, the Viognier, Cabernet-Sauvignon, the Merlot and the Syrah (which is being cultivated more and more on the island). There has also been a resurgence of red vines on the east coast of the island in the Catania region. The happy outcome of these new wine growing and winemaking techniques is the ability to create wines that are distinctively Sicilian, even if they are blended with world-class wines. Within the next decade, the Sicilian wine growing industry will be something to keep an eye on. It's incredible to imagine that such a hot country, where the wine quality once left something to be desired, would one day produce wines of international repute. *Bravissimo* to all the Sicilian wine makers for their perseverance and long-term vision!

As you stroll through Sicilian markets, so greedily will your senses sing at the smell of meat on the grill. Even if *carne* has never been as popular as fish in Sicily, it truly quells your craving when it is well prepared.

Scaloppine alla Siciliana
SICILIAN VEAL ESCALOPES

SERVES 4

4 veal escalopes (5 oz/140 g each)

4 tablespoons (60 ml) flour

1 tablespoon (15 ml) butter

6 tablespoons (90 ml) extra virgin olive oil

Sea salt and pepper to taste

1 onion, finely chopped

1 cup (250 ml) tomato sauce

1 cup (250 ml) white wine

1 tablespoon (15 ml) oregano (fresh or dry)

2 tablespoons (30 ml) fresh basil

Dip the escalopes in flour and brown them in butter with 3 tablespoons (45 ml) of olive oil, while seasoning them with salt and pepper. Set the meat aside on an oven dish. In the same frying pan, brown the onion in the remaining olive oil and add the tomato sauce, white wine, oregano and basil. Pour the sauce over the escalopes and place the dish in a preheated oven (325 °F/160 °C) for 10 minutes. Serve.

Scaloppine al Marsala
VEAL ESCALOPES WITH MARSALA

SERVES 4

4 veal escalopes (5 oz/140 g each)

4 tablespoons (60 ml) flour

1 tablespoon (15 ml) butter

3 tablespoons (45 ml) extra virgin olive oil

1 cup (250 ml) Marsala

Sea salt and pepper to taste

Dip the escalopes in flour and brown them in butter and olive oil. Remove the escalopes from the frying pan before deglazing it with Marsala. Add salt and pepper. Let the sauce breathe for a few minutes and serve it on the escalopes.

Marsala is a fortified wine that owes its name to that picturesque city located in the western part of Sicily. The Arabs called it Marsh'Allah, *which means God's port. Commercialized by Englishman John Woodhouse around 1770, Marsala remained the most exported product in Sicily for two hundred years. More often used for cooking than for drinking, this wine with the heady aroma has finally been getting some proper recognition in the last few years. A few wineries such as Pellegrino, Florio and de Bartoli produce Marsalas of exceptional quality that are reminiscent of Spain's xérès and Portugal's Porto.*

Coniglio all'agrodolce
SWEET AND SOUR RABBIT

This agrodolce *sauce comes from Islamic Persia. During the IXth century, when the Arabs came to Sicily, they brought the secret of sweet and sour sauce with them. It has imparted its special flavor and aroma to a number of dishes that Sicilian families are still wild about today.*

SERVES 4 TO 6

1 rabbit 2 ¾ lbs (1.3 kg), cut into pieces

4 cups (1 liter) white wine

2 onions, finely chopped

4 tablespoons (60 ml) parsley, chopped

2 sprigs thyme

2 bay leaves

6 cloves

Sea salt and pepper

¾ cups (180 ml) white wine vinegar

2 tablespoons (30 ml) sugar

3 tablespoons (45 ml) pine nuts

3 ½ tablespoons (50 ml) currants

Marinate the rabbit pieces with the wine, onion, parsley, thyme, bay leaves, cloves, salt and pepper for 3 hours. Drain the rabbit pieces but keep the marinade and remove the onions. In a large cast iron pot, brown the onions and then the rabbit pieces; pour on half of the marinade and cook uncovered for about 90 minutes over medium heat until the marinade reduces. Add marinade during the cooking process as needed. Ten minutes before it is done, add the vinegar, sugar, pine nuts and currants. Cover the pot and finish cooking the meat. The rabbit meat must be tender, not pink, and fall off the bone easily.

Agnello al forno
ROAST LAMB

SERVES 6

2 lbs (1 kg) shoulder of lamb, cut into pieces

½ cup (125 ml) extra virgin olive oil

Sea salt and pepper to taste

7 oz (200 g) cultivated mushrooms, finely chopped

7 oz (200 g) red and yellow peppers, cut into strips

1 onion, finely sliced

2 cloves garlic, minced

2 sprigs rosemary

1 ½ cups (375 ml) white wine

Rosemary or parsley to decorate

Brown the lamb pieces in olive oil, adding salt and pepper in the process. When it is done, place the meat in a roasting pan along with the mushrooms, peppers, onion, garlic and rosemary. Roast in a preheated oven (400 °F/200 °C) and douse periodically with some of the white wine. After 25 minutes, turn the lamb pieces over and pour on the rest of the wine. Cook for another 25 minutes or until the lamb is nice and tender.

Garnish with rosemary or parsley.

In Sicily, male lambs are castrated, which makes for more flavorful meat.

Filetti di maiale con arance e miele
FILLETS OF PORK WITH ORANGE AND HONEY SAUCE

Pork meat is prized by the Sicilians in the province of Enna and in the city of Ragusa.

SERVES 4 TO 6

2 pork fillets (1 lb/450 g each)

4 tablespoons (60 ml) extra virgin olive oil

2 onions, finely chopped

2 oranges, peeled and cut into pieces

2 sprigs fresh thyme

2 sprigs fresh rosemary

1 ½ cups (375 ml) white wine

3 tablespoons (45 ml) honey

Zest from one orange

Sea salt and pepper to taste

In a frying pan, brown the pork fillets with the onions, oranges, thyme and rosemary. When done, deglaze the frying pan with white wine. Transfer to a roasting pan and cook in a preheated oven at 230 °C (450 °F) for 20 minutes. Remove the fillets and set aside. Take the juice from the dripping pan and reduce it for 5 minutes. Add the honey and zest. Season with salt and pepper.

*The sea… compassionate yet ruthless… peaceful yet wild…
voluptuous yet unyielding. Still unchanged after thousands
of years, the ocean engenders life, hones the landscapes
and delights the islanders.*

CANNOLI

YIELDS 12 CANNOLI

Shell:

3 full tablespoons (50 ml) Marsala

2 tablespoons (30 ml) cocoa

1 egg

5 oz (150 g) flour

2 tablespoons (30 ml) butter

2 tablespoons (30 ml) sugar

1 cup (250 ml) extra virgin olive oil

Filling:

14 oz (400 g) ricotta

5 oz (150 g) sugar

4 tablespoons (60 ml) dark chocolate, crumbled

Mix the shell ingredients, minus the olive oil, until you obtain a fairly firm dough. Spread it out with a rolling pin. Roll the dough around metal or wood cylinders*, taking care to seal the top ends of the dough with a bit of water.

Pour the olive oil into a frying pan. Once it is hot, immerse the dough-covered cylinders. Once they are golden brown, remove them from the oil, drain and cool. Remove the cylinders taking care not to break the shell.

Take a whisk and beat the *ricotta* and sugar until you obtain a smooth, creamy texture. Add the crumbled chocolate and then stuff the *cannoli.*

Refrigerate before serving.

* Metal cannoli *cylinders can be bought in kitchen shops.*

Although considered a carnivaleresque dessert, cannoli *is still one of Sicily's most traditional pastries. Its flavorful, creamy-sweet taste is the delicious result of the* joie de vivre *characteristic of this Mediterranean island.*

CASSATA

SERVES 6 TO 8

Sponge cake:

4 yolks and 2 egg whites

7 oz (200 g) sugar

1 packet Pan Degli Angeli yeast (or 1 ½ tablespoons/22.5 ml baking powder)

1 teaspoon (5 ml) vanilla

7 oz (200 g) flour

7 oz (200 g) melted butter

Beat the eggs and sugar together. Add the yeast or baking powder and the vanilla. Then add the flour and melted butter.

Pour the mixture into a cake mold (approximately 9 in./22 cm in diameter) greased with butter and floured. Bake for about 15 minutes in a preheated oven (375 °F/ 190 °C). Check that the cake is ready with a toothpick: it should come out dry. Turn off the oven and leave the cake inside for about 5 minutes.

Cassata:

7 oz (200 g) green almond paste* (optional)

1 lb (500 g) ricotta

1 lb (500 g) icing sugar

1 lb (500 g) assorted candied fruits*

3.5 oz (100 g) dark chocolate chips

Water

* You can get green almond paste and candied fruit in bakeries or Italian pastry shops.

Cut the sponge cake and green almond paste into small rectangles and alternate them in a cake mold with a detachable bottom. Set aside. Mix the *ricotta* with 7 oz (200 g) sugar, ½ lb (250 g) finely cut candied fruits and the chocolate. Pour this mixture over the sponge cake and green almond paste. Mix some water with the rest of the icing sugar in order to obtain a smooth and creamy texture. Spread this mixture over the *cassata*. Decorate with the rest of the candied fruits.

Surrounded here by typical Sicilian antique porcelain, cassata has always been a traditional offering for Easter and Christmas that is served nowadays at birthdays and other festive occasions. A document dating back to the Mazara Synode of 1575 describes the cassata as a kind of festive dessert. The most famous ones originate from the Valverde monastery in Palermo.

*A carnival treat by virtue
of the pyramid arrangement so
typical of the Ragusa region.*

The San Giorgio church in Ragusa.

PIGNULATA

SERVES 6

9 oz (250 g) flour

2 tablespoons (30 ml) melted butter

2 tablespoons (30 ml) semi-sweet Marsala or cognac

2 eggs

7 oz (200 g) icing sugar

6 tablespoons (90 ml) honey

Virgin olive oil

Zest from one orange (to decorate)

Mix all the ingredients, except for the honey, sugar, olive oil and orange zest. Don't work the dough too much or it will loose its flexibility. Cover with plastic film and set aside for 20 minutes. Roll the dough to obtain a cylinder the width of a grissini (about ½ in./ 1 cm) and cut into pieces 1 in. (2 cm) long. Fry in olive oil heated to 285 °F (140 °C) until the dough is golden brown. Place the fried pieces on a paper towel.

In a saucepan, dissolve the honey and sugar to obtain a syrup. Pour this over the Pignulata, add the orange zest and mix well. Build the pyramid.

Trionfo di San Francesco
SAINT FRANCIS' TRIUMPH

SERVES 4 TO 6

4 empty cannoli shells (see page 103)*

1 lb (450 g) ricotta

7 oz (200 g) sugar

Hazelnut cream (such as Nutella)

3.5 oz (100 g) dark chocolate chips

Crumble the *cannoli* shells. Mix all the ingredients together. Make individual portions out of the mixture. Decorate, according to your whim, with hazelnut cream and crumbled chocolate.

You can buy empty cannoli *shells in Italian pastry shops.*

A big hit with the local clientele, this recipe is an original creation of the Antica Focacceria San Francesco in Palermo.

Sfinci di San Giuseppe
SAINT JOSEPH'S SPHINX

This sweet was created on the east coast of Sicily to commemorate the feast of Saint Joseph. The basic recipe resembles our classic cream puff. The difference is in the ricotta, which adds a quintessential Sicilian touch.

YIELDS 8 TO 10 SMALL DOUGHNUTS

Dough:

¾ cup (180 ml) water

2 tablespoons (30 ml) butter

½ teaspoon (2.5 ml) salt

3.5 oz (100 g) all-purpose flour

3 eggs

1 teaspoon (5 ml) vanilla

1 to 2 cups (250 to 500 ml) extra virgin olive oil

In a saucepan, boil the water with the butter and salt. Add the flour and mix well. Remove from the heat and leave to cool. When the mix has completely cooled, add the eggs, taking care that these are well absorbed by the dough, which should become smooth.

Heat the oil to 325 °F (160 °C). Lower the dough one tablespoon at a time into the oil so that you get a batch of small doughnuts. Fry until golden brown. Leave to cool.

Cream filling:

1 lb (500 g) ricotta

½ lb (250 g) caster sugar

3.5 oz (100 g) dark chocolate chips

Zest from one orange

Pistachios, unsalted and finely chopped

Candied cherries

Mix the *ricotta*, sugar and chocolate. Make a cut in the doughnuts and fill them with the cream mixture. Decorate with pistachios and a cherry.

Cassatelle alla ricotta
RICOTTA HALF-MOONS

YIELDS 8 TO 10 HALF-MOONS

Shells:

10 oz (300 g) flour

1 egg

5 oz (150 g) softened butter

2 tablespoons (30 ml) sugar

Zest from one orange

Zest from one lemon

1 pinch of salt

6 tablespoons (90 ml) water

Combine all the ingredients and knead the dough until it is nice and smooth. Cover with aluminum foil and refrigerate for 30 minutes.

Cream filling:

10 oz (300 g) ricotta

5 oz (150 g) sugar

3 oz (80 g) dark chocolate crumbled into small chunks

1 beaten egg white

Extra virgin olive oil

2 tablespoons (30 ml) icing sugar

½ teaspoon (2.5 ml) cinnamon

In a ceramic dish, mix the *ricotta*, sugar and chocolate.

Spread the dough in a circle 1/16 in. (2 mm) thick. Cut out 3 in. (8 cm) diameter circles. In the center of each one, place one teaspoon of the *ricotta* cream filling. Using a brush, apply egg white to the dough edges and then fold into half-moon shapes.

Fry the half-moons in the olive oil for one minute, turning them over with two spatulas. Drain and place on paper towels. As soon as they are cooled, sprinkle on the caster sugar and cinnamon.

These wonderfully delicious little cakes were photographed at Club Posta Ponente, in Capo Gallo, 15 km west of Palermo.

Crema di anguria
WATERMELON CREAM

SERVES 4

2 cups (½ liter) watermelon juice

7 oz (200 g) sugar

3 drops essence of jasmine (optional)

5 tablespoons (75 ml) cornstarch

1 teaspoon (5 ml) cinnamon

Crumbled chocolate

Pistachios, unsalted and finely chopped

Blend watermelon pieces separately until you get 2 cups (½ liter) of juice. In a saucepan, put the watermelon juice, sugar, essence of jasmine and cornstarch. Cook over low heat and stir until boiling. Lower the heat and cook, while stirring, for 4 to 5 minutes. Remove from the heat, add the cinnamon and set aside. Pour in ramekins or in a large bowl. Decorate with chocolate and pistachios.

This refreshing dessert is served in honor of the feast of Saint Rosalie, the patron saint of Palermo, from July 11th to the 15th, and on September 4th.

Gelatina di limone
LEMON JELLY

SERVES 4

¾ cup (180 ml) water

7 oz (200 g) sugar

¾ cup (180 ml) lemon juice

5 tablespoons (75 ml) starch or cornstarch

1 packet powdered gelatin

Zest from one lemon

Pistachios, unsalted and finely chopped

Place all ingredients in a saucepan, except for the gelatin, the zest and the pistachios. Cook over low heat and stir until boiling. Remove from the heat and add the gelatin while continuing to stir. Pour into a large bowl and let cool. Decorate with lemon zest and pistachios.

Bianco mangiare
BLANCMANGE

In XIVth century France, blancmange was mainly served to the sick and to women who had recently given birth. It was the monzù, *French chefs hired by Palermo's aristocracy, who brought this dish to Sicily, a recipe still highly appreciated by Sicilian families. There are many existing versions, but white cream and almonds are always part of the basic make-up.*

SERVES 6

4 cups (1 liter) milk

7oz (200 g) sugar

½ cup (125 ml) flour

6 tablespoons (90 ml) powdered almonds

2 tablespoons (50 g) butter

2 ½ teaspoons (12.5 ml) cornstarch

2 drops almond extract

Splintered dark chocolate

Place all the ingredients, except for the chocolate, in a saucepan and bring to a gentle boil while stirring. Once the liquid becomes velvety smooth, remove from the heat. Pour into small containers and set aside to cool. Refrigerate. Sprinkle with chocolate chips before serving.

Granita di caffè
COFFEE GRANITA

SERVES 6

2 cups (500 ml) boiling water

7 oz (200 g) sugar

½ cup (125 ml) hot black coffee

1 cup (250 ml) whipping cream

Icing sugar

In a bowl, mix the sugar, water and coffee. Place it in the freezer for 3 to 4 hours, stirring it every 30 minutes so that the liquid does not solidify. Remove from the freezer about 40 minutes before serving. Apply a dollop of whipping cream (whipped with the icing sugar).

Granita *is very refreshing during heat waves.*

Gelato di pistacchio
PISTACHIO
ICE CREAM

In the center of Palermo, via Notarbartollo, Giovanni Stancampiano, one of the most reputed ice cream makers in the city, has been making the same gelati for 25 years and now has more than 40 flavors. The secret of his success is that he only uses high quality, natural ingredients. His "ice cream" contains neither eggs nor cream, just milk and fresh fruit. A real treat in the heat!

YIELDS ABOUT 1 LITER

10 oz (300 g) sugar

1 tablespoon (15 ml) cornstarch

4 cups (1 liter) milk

3.5 oz (100 g) buttermilk*

7 oz (200 g) salted pistachios, finely chopped

* Buttermilk is just that, the milky product that's left after the cream is churned.

Mix the sugar with the cornstarch and set aside. Heat the milk over low heat. Add the buttermilk and the sugar/cornstarch recipe. Cook over low heat while stirring continuously. Once the liquid thickens, remove from the heat and add the pistachios. Leave to cool. Place in the freezer or in an ice cream maker.

If you prefer strawberry ice cream, use the same quantities for all the ingredients except the milk (you'll need 5 cups/1 ⅓ liters of milk) and replace the pistachios with 10 oz (300 g) of strawberries.

The birth of Sicilian ice cream began with sherbet. When the Arabs arrived in the IXth century, they taught the Sicilians how to make sherbet by first collecting the ice on the peak of Mount Etna. The ice was crushed, then mixed with fruit juice. Over the course of the centuries, mainly due to the progress of refrigeration techniques, islanders began manufacturing ice cream. Sicilian gelati is renowned not only throughout Italy, but in the rest of the western world as well. Is it the best in the world? In Sicily, they will surely reply a resounding "yes"!

In Sicily, ice cream is so popular, people even eat it in the morning. This bun filled with pistachio ice cream is a classic breakfast dish.

Almond paste

Planted by the Arabs, almond trees abound in Sicily. The nut is used to add flavor to a variety of fish and meat dishes but it is mostly used in desserts such as cakes, cookies, nougat and candies. Created in the XIVth century by Héloïse Martorana, founder of the Benedictine order in Palermo, almond paste was christened *Frutta di Martorana* in her honor. Some of the almond paste fruit seen in bakery windows are so faithfully reproduced they look like the real thing. Almond paste is also used to make almond milk: all you have to do is put some almond paste and water into a blender and mix well. Served in many Sicilian bars, this smooth, sweet drink is highly appreciated during a heat wave.

Viva Maria!

Sicily owes a lot to Maria Grammatico who was responsible for the rebirth of the Sicilian pastry-making tradition. In 1950, she was sent to an orphanage run by the Franciscans in Erice, a quasi-mediaeval village perched on a hillside on the west coast of Sicily. The nuns taught Maria how to prepare the pastries that were sold outside the convent. Once she left the convent, her pastry making talent led her to open a bakery shop in Erice where cakes, all kinds of cookies and *cassata* were eagerly received by the public. In this photograph, she is holding a dish of *Mostaccioli*, typical Christmas cakes made with almonds and nuts. Maria preferred to keep the recipe a secret.

Between Tiziana and Magda, the author Janine Saine.

The Palermo Team

Under a sun reaching temperatures as high as 95 °F (35 °C), we succeeded (without too many snags!) in producing the visuals for these Sicilian recipes. As I remember the *momentum* of our conversations — which were interspersed with Italian song and some English too — I would like to say (in my first language, French!): *mille fois bravo et merci à* (Bravo a thousand times, and thanks to):

Pucci Scafidi, renowned Palermo photographer whose father and grandfather practiced the same art in this city as well as throughout Sicily;

Francesco Pedone, Assistant Photographer;

Tiziana Romeo, Culinary Designer;

Magda Serafini, renowned Artistic Director (photographs) in Palermo.

Opposite page: In the enchanting San Elia site, this seaside composition illustrates the Sicilian "joie de vivre"

"...and I saw an old man in Virzi bend down to touch the land, shaping its contours with his fingers. I saw the colors of a natural and human order come together in time, as a simple but real tale. I saw blue light extending high in the sky as well as pressing the ground, softly, in shade and ochre. Of these places, vivid is the memory, so it is the emotion from its scents and sounds. This is the soul of Virzi..."

FRANCESCO SPADAFORA

Situated on the west coast of Sicily, 60 kilometers south of Palermo, Virzi is a place where the hills are so lush with fruit trees, olive groves, wheat fields and vines, they emanate an almost biblical quality.

National Library of Canada Cataloguing in Publication

Saine, Janine
Sicily: a way of life in 50 recipes
Translation of: La Sicile: un art de vivre en 50 recettes.
ISBN 2-89455-134-7
1. Cookery, Italian - Sicilian style. 2. Sicily (Italy). I. Title.
TX723.2.S55S2413 2003   641.59458   C2003-940559-1

The Publisher gratefully acknowledges the financial aid of the Government of
Canada through the Book Publishing Industry Development Program as well as the
assistance received from SODEC for our publishing activities.

 Patrimoine canadien / Canadian Heritage   Canadä   SODEC Québec

Graphic Design: Christiane Séguin
Translation: Jane Davey
Editing: Pierre-Yves Le Dilicocq and Françoise Périllat
Recipe photographs: Pucci Scafidi
Ambiance photography: Janine Saine
Photographs on p. 37, 44 and 91: Nicola Scafidi, Pucci Scafidi's father
Photographs on p. 87 (top left) and 88 (top right): Letterio Pomara and
Donnafugata
Photographs on p. 87 (to the right): Planeta

Legal Deposit second quarter 2003
Bibliothèque Nationale du Québec and the National Library of Canada
ISBN 2-89455-134-7

Green Frog Publishing is an imprint of Guy Saint-Jean Éditeur inc.
3154, boul. Industriel, Laval (Québec) Canada H7L 4P7.
Tel. (450) 663-1777. Fax: (450) 663-6666.
E-Mail: saint-jean.editeur@qc.aira.com   Web: www.saint-jeanediteur.com

Printed and bound in Singapore